I

JOSNEY RODRÍGUEZ

FRUSTRATED
LEADERS
NO MORE!
LIFELESS
CHURCHES

Secrets to experience the kingdom of God in your leadership.

Title: No More Frustrated Leaders and Lifeless Churches

Subtitle: Secrets to experiencing the kingdom of God in your leadership

Series: Empowered

Text editing and Cover

Josney Rodríguez

ISBN: 979-8-34535-636-4

All Bible quotations in this book are taken from the *New King James Version,* unless otherwise noted.

1st edition: November 2024

Printed independently for academic purposes.

Dedication

To God, who makes all things possible.

CONTENT

No more frustrated leaders and lifeless churches

INTRODUCTION

Frustration in leadership is neither a strange nor uncommon emotion.[1] On the contrary, it is like dark, stormy days—an inevitable part of the climate of our life on earth. It happens often. However, true leaders strive to ensure that the sunny days of victories achieved appear more frequently in the atmospheric landscape as they carry out their work.

In a way, disappointment is an inherent part of the administrative journey. Those who genuinely take on the responsibility of doing their best, achieving the most, and driving transformation will inevitably face a series of obstacles: uncertainty, resistance to change, and lack of commitment. These are some of the circumstances where frustration tends to emerge.[2]

Now, while it is understandable and even tolerable that, in the beginning, one may lack the necessary capabilities to achieve significant change, what is unacceptable and inadmissible is failing to take full responsibility for the outcomes. Why?

---

[1] One of the clearest examples of leadership fighting resistance to change on the part of its collaborators is Jesus (Matthew 17:17; Mark 9:19, 24; Luke 9:41).

[2]Jane Hunt, 100 Biblical Keys to Counseling (Dallas, TX: Hope for the Heart, 1990–2011), 15, discusses a leadership experience related to frustration in the life of Moses (Numbers 20:1-12): "Moses He was so frustrated that his anger reached its maximum level. Instead of speaking to the rock, he hit it...twice. God wanted an explosion of water, not an explosion of anger. The result was that the Lord had to discipline his chosen leader and not allow her to introduce his people to the Promised Land."

The answer is simple: a true leader must embrace a teleological commitment to their role.[3] In other words, there is an end goal or objective that must be accomplished as a result of their efforts. A leader must understand that their leadership finds its meaning and value in the achievement and realization of the proposed goals or objectives.

In Christ's response to Pilate, the teleological vision of His leadership is expressed with great clarity: "You say rightly that I am a king. For this cause I was born, and for this cause I have come into the world, that I should bear witness to the truth. Everyone who is of the truth hears My voice." (John 18:37).[4]

On the other hand, the ontological understanding[5] of leadership reveals that leadership is a driving force for mobilizing and inspiring individuals. In this

---

[3] The word *teleological* indeed has its roots in the Greek word *telos*, meaning "end" or "purpose." When we discuss the *teleological concept of leadership*, we are focusing on leadership by its ultimate purpose or goal. This approach means defining leadership not merely by the actions taken or the role itself, but by the intended outcomes or the greater purpose that leadership seeks to fulfill. In other words, a teleological perspective on leadership emphasizes leading with a clear vision of the ultimate goals, guiding principles, and the end impact one aims to achieve.

[4] John the Baptist, Paul, and each of the disciples knew perfectly well the purpose of their leadership (John 1:32; Galatians 2:7; Matthew 28:18-20). A deeper understanding of what biblical leadership means and its challenges can be found in my book Transformative Leadership: Secrets of Christian Discipleship (Doral, FL: IADPA, 2023), in chapter 1: What do you expect from your leadership?

[5] An *ontological* view indeed focuses on the *nature* or *essence* of something. In terms of leadership, an ontological perspective centers on understanding what leadership fundamentally *is*, rather than just what it accomplishes or the goals it aims to achieve. This view seeks to define leadership by its inherent qualities, values, and characteristics, exploring the underlying nature of what it means to be a leader. It looks at the essence of leadership—what makes leadership *leadership*—and emphasizes understanding the intrinsic attributes that distinguish true leadership at its core.

sense, leadership is not just about completing tasks; it is also about influencing people. A leader operates through others. Given this, it is reasonable to conclude that, as a leader, you must possess the ability to inspire others to achieve the desired objectives or goals. This challenge of influencing others can lead to frustration if you are unable to motivate them and secure their commitment to the task.

To fully grasp the complexities of leadership from various perspectives and evaluate the reasons behind its significant challenges—and, consequently, its frustrations—we must also consider leadership from a theological perspective.[6]

Walking the path of theology allows us to see beyond the humanistic ideas that have permeated even conceptions of biblical leadership in the contemporary world. Few have noticed it, but the humanist worldview—fed by rationalist philosophical ideas—has influenced modern spiritual leadership, stripping it of its power and purpose.

A leadership that focuses solely on what humans can accomplish through their own strength and abilities, while ignoring or obscuring the reality of God's presence in fulfilling His purposes through leadership, weakens faith and diminishes the role of churches and their leaders. From a biblical worldview, leadership has a divine role, with an eternal purpose closely tied to fulfilling God's will, regardless of the obstacles or challenges faced. In this context, if

---

[6]The word *theology* indeed relates to the study of God, exploring divine attributes, purposes, and will. When considering the biblical worldview of leadership, it's essential to delve into both the *purpose* and *nature* of leadership as understood from God's perspective. This means examining leadership not merely as a human role or social function but as a divinely ordained responsibility, rooted in God's intentions and aligned with His will. Leadership, from this perspective, involves qualities such as service, humility, and stewardship, all grounded in a commitment to God's principles and purposes. This theological approach provides a foundation for leadership that aligns with a spiritual calling and divine guidance, distinguishing it from purely secular views of leadership.

11

frustration stems from human inability, we must ask: is anything impossible for God? (Genesis 18:14-16, Jeremiah 32:27, Luke 1:37).

Even when we encounter difficulties or feel inadequate, we can trust that God has the power to overcome any obstacle, working beyond our understanding and abilities to accomplish His purposes through us, including in leadership.

The dominance of humanism, which shapes many sociological constructs, needs to be not merely compared but confronted with the biblical model of leadership as presented in the Word of God—leadership that fulfills divine purpose and achieves true success. Therefore, the material you now hold is crafted primarily from this worldview. God's vision and His relationship with leadership are the foundational aspects of successful spiritual leadership.

Yet, reality shows that many leaders, even in spiritual contexts, have not experienced the fullness of God's promises in their lives. As a result, preparing a manual for such leaders is both necessary and urgent. You, I, and every person called by God to fulfill a task and influence others need the opportunity to learn the four most important principles for success in leadership. You need a compass, a map of the territory, and, why not, a travel itinerary.

In the introduction to his book *21 Lessons for the 21st Century*,[7] Israeli author Yuval Noah Harari states, "In a world deluged by irrelevant information, clarity is power." My hope is that divine knowledge concerning leadership and personal formation will impact many who are seeking answers to their struggles and frustrations in church leadership. The time has come to apply the principles that God has outlined for the success of His kingdom on earth.

---

[7] Yuval Noah Harari, 21 lessons for the 21st century (Barcelona, Spain: Penguin Random House Grupo Editorial, 2018).

1

The Leader's Challenge: TURNING GOALS INTO ACHIEVEMENTS

Since childhood, I have lived near the sea. Whenever I stood before that vast, endless expanse of water stretching out before my eyes, I could feel its indomitable power, its inscrutable wisdom, and its unreachable boundaries. Can the sea be something I control or predict?

When I contemplate the challenge of leadership, I find this analogy with the sea deeply inspiring. If we underestimate the sea, we risk being swallowed by its depths, deprived of breath and struggling to survive. In much the same way, the exercise of leadership immerses us in an abyss of responsibilities and challenges. It is not enough to simply float; we must swim with strength and determination to reach our destination.

I believe that the greatest hindrance to churches and organizations lies in two critical aspects: first, the true nature of leadership is underestimated; and second, even worse, there is a lack of clarity about what leadership truly means. Let's take time to address these two crucial points in order to steer ourselves toward the path of effective leadership.

I am confident that the desire to grow and succeed in the practice of leadership resides in the hearts of those who read this book and sincerely believe that achieving success in leadership is indeed possible.

The Problem of Underestimating Leadership

Suggesting that one of the main issues with leadership is its underestimation might surprise some. How can we be underestimating leadership? To underestimate something means failing to recognize its true value. In other words, leadership has been pushed into a secondary—or sometimes nonexistent—role within the complex dynamics of organizations.

Understanding its importance is key to illuminating the path toward success and driving congregational transformation. On the other hand, those who downplay the role of leadership will find it difficult to progress—or even survive.

Let me share three clear signs that indicate leadership is being undervalued.

Leaders unaware of their weaknesses. Often, when organizations are evaluated, the focus tends to be on external factors, while one of the most critical elements for congregational growth—leadership—is either overlooked or underestimated. It is essential to remember that the growth of a church is directly tied to the development of its leaders' capacity to lead. When the weaknesses that hinder or limit a leader's influence go unrecognized, an invisible ceiling is placed over the church, preventing the transformation one seeks to achieve.

Leaders who neither grow themselves nor help others develop leadership skills. One of the most notable weaknesses in leadership is the lack of personal growth and the inability to cultivate leadership skills in others. Additionally, the absence of an intentional development plan is a serious concern. When no leadership training program is in place, it sends a clear message that leadership is being undervalued within the congregation. However, by giving proper attention to this area, substantial growth within the church can be achieved.

Ineffective Leaders Contribute to the Downfall of Organizations. One of the most serious consequences of underestimating leadership is the collapse of organizations. It's like a patient who fails to recover—clearly, the treatment is ineffective. In the same way, when problems within a congregation persist unresolved, it signals that the leadership strategies in place may be inadequate. Witnessing an organization that is "taking on water" is a clear indication that leadership must become a priority.

By assessing these areas, we gain insight into how the church and its leaders value leadership. These three symptoms can be distilled into three fundamental questions: Who are we? What are we doing? And what are the growth results of the organization?

An illustration of this truth

The story of Saul serves as a relevant example in the analysis of leadership. Who was Saul? What was his most significant weakness that undermined his leadership? Scripture reveals that Saul prioritized pleasing himself and his people over pleasing God. His self-sufficiency and independence from God became his downfall. What was he doing? His actions were driven by a desire for self-exaltation. He felt threatened by the success and growth of other leaders, and his pride was wounded when others received more recognition. Worst of all, he was unwilling to change or grow.

What were the results? The defeat of his beloved people. The Philistines won a crucial battle, costing the lives of the king and his children. Is there a more catastrophic defeat than this? Hardly. The root cause of this tragedy was Saul's underestimation of the importance of a leader who recognizes his weaknesses, strives for change, seeks growth, and helps others do the same. Moreover, a successful leader produces tangible achievements as a result of their work.

In contrast, consider David's leadership. Although far from perfect—he committed sins as grievous as, or even worse than, Saul's—David sincerely acknowledged his mistakes and his need for growth. The key difference is that, despite our failures, leadership is strengthened when we accept the need for change and are willing to transform. Let us not forget the incredible power God pours out when a leader becomes a living example of transformation.

David stands as an inspiring model of leadership. Unlike Saul, he was willing to change. One of the clearest examples was when he heeded the advice of Abigail, Nabal's wife. His psalms further demonstrate his desire for personal growth and improvement in his leadership. He continually sought to move forward in alignment with God's plan. This was no minor matter—when God told him he wouldn't build the temple, he humbly accepted it. David's willingness to change, improve, and grow became evident in his leadership.

The results were extraordinary. Under David's reign, the people experienced a glorious period in history. In contrast to the defeat under Saul, David's victories over the Philistines and other enemies were constant and remarkable.

Underestimating leadership is a common mistake in many congregations, leading to much pain and frustration. However, investing in leadership development is crucial. The return on this investment is disproportionate: dedicating 20% of time to leadership generates 80% of the results. Without well-prepared leaders, transformation is impossible.

Would you like to try this approach? When I grasped this principle, I stopped underestimating leadership—both in my own life and within the congregation. I stopped blaming poor results on a lack of qualified people to work or lead. Years passed, and leaders came and went, yet the results remained stagnant. Why would anything change?

Transformation begins with leaders who are willing to grow and empower others. If we expect the congregation to embrace change, the leader must lead the charge. In the following chapters, we will explore this key principle for the success of any community.

Have you ever felt exhausted from being the only person you can rely on? This must change. In the next chapters of this book, particularly in chapter 5, we will delve into how this principle of leadership transformation is fulfilled.[8]

I am encouraged to see that, in certain places, church leaders have embraced this important truth and are dedicating more time to developing leaders. Some universities have even begun offering graduate programs and doctorates in leadership, which is clear evidence of the growing recognition of its importance in our time, particularly when it comes to guiding organizations to higher levels of success.

The problem of not understanding the true meaning of leadership

Underestimating leadership often results in a lack of clarity about what it truly means to be a leader. It's like looking up definitions in a dictionary that doesn't provide the correct meanings. Sadly, the absence of leadership training has caused many pastors and congregational leaders to pursue abstract concepts, illusions, and false expectations in their attempts to lead.

I remember when I experienced this myself. I had been taught how to study the Bible, prepare sermons, preach, and organize programs. Yet, I didn't have a clear understanding of what it truly meant to be a leader. I was anxious and unsure about how to engage and motivate people. I thought perhaps I didn't know the right plan. I worked tirelessly, searching for that "treasure" that would transform my ministry. My library filled with books, but the answers continued to elude me.

---

[8] I would also recommend using my other books: *Dream Big: Leadership That Make the Difference* (Doral, FL: IADPA, 2019) and Leadership That Transforms: Secrets of Christian Discipleship (Doral, FL: IADPA, 2023).

One day, as I was browsing through the aisles of a bookstore, I stumbled upon a leadership book by John Maxwell. As I read it, something shifted within me. My thoughts lit up, and I realized:

The problem isn't the programs or events I'm organizing, The problem is that I don't understand what it means to be a manager or leader.

This thought planted a seed that took root in my mind. Thus began my long journey in search of the deeper meaning of leadership. The frustration I had felt as a leader started to fade. My ministry was transformed! The churches I led embarked on a path toward limitless growth.[9]

Today, dear reader, as you hold this book in your hands and eagerly absorb its content, I know that you share the same burning desire to leave behind the path of stagnation and lack of motivation among your members. My prayer is that this material will accompany you on your own journey of growth as a leader.

To truly understand leadership, it's important to begin by recognizing what leadership is NOT. Think of it as viewing the negative of a photograph—by identifying what leadership isn't, we can better define and highlight the true outlines of what leadership IS, especially in the ecclesiastical field.

1. Leadership *is not* simply about knowing how to preach.

We certainly agree on the conviction that preaching is a vital part of pastoral work. The exposition of the Word deeply impacts hearts and prepares the human spirit to follow God. However, being a skilled preacher does not automatically make someone an effective leader.

---

[9]The principles that will be shown in the following chapters are divine tools for congregations to travel the path of the apostolic church, in whose description Luke speaks of adding people every day, multiplying and growing in the Word of God.

At the beginning of my ministry, I was focused on improving my preaching. I bought books, studied diligently, and worked hard, believing that this was the key to successful leadership. While my preaching began to improve, I soon realized it wasn't enough. I lacked the skills to lead, motivate people, and bring about meaningful change in the congregation.

In three consecutive districts, I encountered painful experiences that made me question my effectiveness as a pastor. Senior leaders in the congregations resisted change and were often unwilling to participate in world church events. They rejected ideas I presented, and even when they approved programs, they didn't participate in carrying them out.

Their comments were discouraging: "Thank you for your sermon," they'd say, followed by remarks like, "We can't implement that program because the members don't like it and won't participate." Another would add, "We've tried it before, and it didn't work," or, "I've been in this church since it was founded, and from my experience, that won't work here."

I continued preaching passionately, hoping things would somehow change. But while they seemed pleased to hear me preach, nothing else changed. If I wanted anything to happen, I had to take on the responsibility of doing everything myself.

I recall one event where everything went wrong. I was embarrassed and deeply disappointed by the outcome. That's when I realized that my sermons alone weren't enough to lead effectively.

Leadership extends far beyond the pulpit. It requires a range of skills: understanding people, motivating them, implementing change, making tough decisions, and working as a team. Fortunately, I learned that becoming a good leader is an ongoing process of growth and development. There's always more to learn and improve.

2. *Leadership **is not** simply about holding a position.*

Sometimes, being appointed to a position is mistakenly seen as equivalent to leadership. Those who hold this view may say, "What I say goes because I'm in charge." However, these individuals fail to realize that leadership extends far beyond a title, position, or rank.

Holding a position doesn't automatically mean people will follow you. Leadership is not an instant result of authority—especially in today's context, where postmodernism has challenged traditional ideas of hierarchy and unquestioned authority. In the past, institutions like the church or government had the final say, but modern congregations operate differently.

Do you see it? Pastors today cannot assume that, simply because they hold the title of lead pastor, parishioners will automatically follow their direction without question.

I recall a church board meeting one Saturday afternoon. I had just started as the new pastor the week before. The meeting was about organizing an upcoming evangelistic campaign set to take place in four weeks. I presented a bold plan for the congregation. One of the elders, an influential doctor, responded with a deep, resonant voice: "Work first, pastor, and we will follow."

Those words have stayed with me, not just because they were memorable, but because they made me reflect. He didn't care at all that I had been appointed as the pastor. I realized then that my leadership wasn't rooted in my title but in my actions. My example was far more important than the position I held.

Dear reader, we don't follow those we don't know. We follow those who set an example for us. We accompany leaders who have demonstrated their ability to lead and take action. In his renowned book, *The Seven Habits of Highly Effective People*,[10] Covey noted that character is a key aspect of successful

---

[10]Stephen R. Covey, The Seven Habits of Highly Effective People (Buenos Aires, Argentina: Paidós, 2003).

eadership. Who we are, as demonstrated by our actions, carries more weight than the position we hold.

3. Leadership *is not* merely about having academic qualifications..

I hung up the phone. It was an old, gray device, finally in my hands for communication. I touched my hands together and sat for a few minutes, lost in thought. I wasn't really present—only physically. Then, I stood up and went to speak with my wife.

"The president called me again," I said slowly. She understood the weight of that word—"again." For the past four months, the president had been calling to ask why the congregations under my care were not growing.

My wife and I had studied theology together, but that wasn't enough. I was feeling frustrated. Four years of study and the honors at graduation had not turned me into a leader.

I realized that having knowledge in several areas and being a professional didn't automatically mean I knew how to lead. Being a specialist does not make someone a leader. Leadership is a specialization in itself. It requires acquiring knowledge, accumulating experiences, and developing skills. And like any other skill, it takes time.

4. Leadership *is not* simply about being under the guidance of a great leader.

It's true that we can serve under the leadership of an exceptional individual and still feel frustrated by the results. While the influence of great leaders can be beneficial, it does not guarantee success if that is what we are seeking. Sometimes smaller boats try to ride the wake of large ships, but while that may provide a temporary boost, it's not enough to reach the intended destination.

It's valuable to represent others and speak on their behalf, but we must also acknowledge the importance of our own influence. If we only say, "Do this because my boss said so," we reveal a lack of self-leadership. In those moments, it's important to remember that the evaluation of outcomes doesn't rest solely on our superior. As leaders, we are accountable for both successes and failures.

If you are the leader, the results you achieve will reflect your own ability to lead, inspire, and make decisions. No matter how large the shadow of previous leaders may be, what truly matters is how you exercise your leadership and how you impact those who follow you.

5. Leadership **is not** simply about having many years of service.

Sometimes there is a collective belief, either consciously or subconsciously, that if someone has many years of service in ministry, they must be a leader. Those who think this way are equating length of service with leadership ability. However, it's important to clarify a few points on this matter.

First, having years of service is not the same as having broad experience. Experience involves facing various situations and applying the skills acquired over time. While it may seem logical that prolonged practice in a role leads to greater expertise, the reality doesn't always align with this assumption.

Experience cannot be taken for granted. We cannot assume that simply having many years of service guarantees the leadership skills necessary to drive growth and change within congregations. Take a moment to look around and reflect on this. Leadership should not be automatically attributed based solely on years of experience.

In my opinion, this issue stems from two key causes. The first is that, in many cases, the years pass without the creation and development of new learning opportunities. The second is the absence of active learning—years of work repeating the same tasks without seeking ways to grow and improve. True leadership involves continuous growth and the ability to positively influence others.

In front of the hospital

I was sitting on the sidewalk, right in the path of pedestrians. I heard the blaring siren of the ambulance as it approached the emergency entrance of the hospital. People were rushing around—some worried, others with tears in their eyes. I don't quite remember why I was there. Maybe I was waiting for someone who had agreed to help me find a place to live. After several weeks in that area, I still hadn't secured a home. But what I do remember clearly are my thoughts.

"Why am I here?" In a very short time, I had already passed through two districts. And now, this was the third. Yes, you heard that right. This place had been a district project for years. The leaders didn't respect the pastor, and the members were divided. Only about three dozen people made up the congregation. For months, I had been separated from my pregnant wife, trying to find a place to live, without success. In that moment, I asked myself, "What does God expect from me?"

I don't know your personal experience, but in my case, when I don't understand God's purpose for my life, I immerse myself in conversation with Him. That reddish afternoon, as the last rays of sunlight faded behind the hospital, without a home, without my wife by my side, without support from leaders, and without money, I found myself in the midst of the stormy sea of leadership. Tossed by the wind and battered by the storm, I stood in the darkness of the unknown.

This chapter of my life, along with others you'll discover, led me to ask some tough questions:

- Am I truly prepared to be a pastor and leader of a congregation?

- If the members don't accept my leadership or want change, what can I do to turn that around?

- What can God do for me and through me in these circumstances?

- What is the secret of a pastor who sees his church transformed?

Divine providence began to work, and every day, for more than 33 years, I have seen God's hand guiding me. Throughout that time, I have tirelessly sought to learn more about how to become more effective and efficient in pastoral leadership. I have faced challenges and attacks from Satan, and many times I've felt alone, standing before the hospital of my own existence, not knowing how to change the situation. I never imagined that years later, God would give me the opportunity to write this book for other ministers, new to leadership, who are facing similar challenges.[11]

Do you know why?

First, because I genuinely care for each one of you, my dear friends, whether pastors or church elders. Second, because I've been in your shoes, and I know how difficult it can be. My sincere mission in life is to help as many ministers as possible, so they can understand, learn, and overcome the arduous path of pastoral leadership with resounding success.

Something must change.

Making the decision to grow in your leadership is the most important choice you can make. This decision will enhance the value of every other quality and gift that God has given you for your life mission.

If you move forward with determination and faith, I am confident that a new, passionate ministry will unfold before you as you learn the four fundamental principles for navigating the sea of uncertainty and complexity that lies beyond your control. Additionally, you will discover how to develop effective strategies to implement in your leadership, resulting in meaningful

---

[11] The decision to prepare myself in pastoral leadership and learn everything that the improvement of this field meant, led me to write the first two articles in the 90s, titled: "The Ministry Aspirant" and "The Pastor Against the success or failure." Today I am happy to share this experience.

change within your congregation. Most importantly, you will experience outcomes you have never seen before. Nothing can bring you more satisfaction and a deeper sense of purpose.

The offer

You may or may not know me, but I want to reaffirm my commitment to supporting you as you apply the principles you are about to learn. My dream goes beyond merely sharing my experiences and knowledge through this book—it's about seeing you experience the incredible results that come from putting these principles into action.

To make this a reality for your ministry, you'll have the opportunity to register online and gain access to additional materials, as well as information about the monthly training sessions we will hold for those implementing these concepts.

Furthermore, we can arrange in-person meetings to train leaders in your region, because growing your leadership and those around you is the first critical step.

Now, more than ever, churches need leaders who truly understand what it means to achieve success. It's vital not to underestimate leadership or misunderstand its true meaning. Instead, we must move forward with a daily commitment to grow our own leadership and to cultivate the leadership of others.

No more frustrated leaders and lifeless churches

2

The spirit of the leader: THE SECRET TO CHANGE

I looked at my watch. It was 4:00 a.m. The sound of snoring filled the room. Should I get up? Yes, I answered myself. The day before, I had visited several church members and had gone to bed late on that thin mat on the second floor of the pastoral quarters (we called it the "upper room"). Naturally, I hadn't slept well. I was still exhausted and wanted to continue sleeping. But I couldn't. The night before, I had made a decision that would mark my ministry.

At the first meeting of the main church, I hadn't been allowed to lead. In every conversation, all I heard were criticisms of former pastors and senior leaders. "This one is too liberal," they said. "That one made poor decisions." "The church didn't want him as pastor." "They don't understand how our church operates." "We only had one good pastor" (that was, of course, an exception). "You're too young and lack experience."

Recently, a pastor asked me, "How can I best fulfill my ministry?" At every meeting I attend, I try to answer this question through Scripture and the spirit of prophecy. As you saw in the previous chapter, I am a firm believer that the key to achieving any form of consecration lies in the quality of leadership. Solomon wisely wrote in the book of Proverbs: "Where there is no vision, the people perish" (Proverbs 29:18, MEV, Modern English Version).

Therefore, the question of how to be a better leader is always present in my mind and heart. Anyone who has taken on responsibilities—whether as a parent, a congregational leader, or a representative of any organization—needs to ask the same question. The reason is simple: leading people and driving change requires far more than good intentions. Would you agree?

Paul put it this way: "So then it is not of him who wills, nor of him who runs, but of God who shows mercy" (Romans 9:16). Many may have the desire, but desire alone is not enough, just as it isn't in other areas of life.

Recently, I heard a specialist mention that while many people venture into leadership roles in companies or organizations, only five percent succeed. Yes, just five percent!

Contrary to what many might believe when starting their leadership journey, in most cases, the outcome becomes either a life lesson or, at best, an opportunity to learn. Someone once said, "The road to failure is paved with good intentions." Between wishing for our dreams and actually realizing them, there lies a challenging and uncertain path.

You hold this book in your hands today because you already know, deep down, that good intentions alone won't lead to success. You feel a stirring excitement for the great things that can happen in your life. And although the journey may be difficult, you're willing to take the next step forward. I celebrate your determination! My hope is that you stay committed to reaching your destiny: becoming the leader God has called you to be.

The start of my leadership journey

Early in my ministry, I was assigned to a small district where the main church had been a group—without official church status—for over eighteen years. Yes, you read that correctly: 18 years! Now, what happens when a congregation goes that long without growth? Have you ever thought about it?

I'm sure you've come across some of these congregations. It's the same group of brothers and sisters, their hair gradually turning white, who remain at the forefront of leadership because the new generation has faded away, and the newly baptized members don't stay.

The furniture, the pews, the pulpit, and the utensils, along with the structure itself—walls and floors—feel like part of an old photograph. Nothing is new. Time has stood still. It's as though everything is frozen in the moment it all began. You might even think the physical place of worship mirrors what is happening in the hearts of the church members. So, what is going on with this congregation?

The purpose of this book is to empower those who carry the great responsibility of leadership and who aim for more than just good intentions. Deep in their souls, in their sincere commitment to God, they long to succeed in their mission, not to fail in their desire, intention, or life purpose. Fulfilling God's plans within their congregations is the reason for their existence.

Dear reader, now I'd like to share with you the first foundational principle for seeing change in your ministry and, naturally, in your congregation. This new beginning emerges from understanding and reflecting on seven key aspects that you must consider to galvanize and ignite your spirit as a leader, and the spirits of those around you. It's the first and most essential step in breaking free from the stagnation of the status quo, the absence of unity, and, of course, the lack of growth.

Take the necessary time to reflect on each of these aspects. While they could each be explored in depth on their own, together they become the spark that will ignite true revival and reformation in your congregation.

1.   Find out what *your opinion* is of the condition of the church.

Think carefully about this: Do you consider the current condition of your church normal or acceptable, either for yourself or for the congregation? Do you believe that change is impossible for your church? Has frustration reached such a point that you think change would only happen through a miracle? These questions are meant for you to answer honestly. It's not about saying what others think is appropriate, but rather expressing what is truly in your heart and in the hearts of your church leaders.

After visiting many churches in various places, I've encountered this same spiritual condition in many congregations. Surprisingly, it used to seem normal to me. I, too, was part of the "furniture"! However, after years in leadership, I began to see things differently. I finally understood the deeper issue. I'm convinced that, at that moment (and I firmly believe it was the Spirit of God enlightening me), I realized that what was happening in these congregations was not just a description or symptom of the problem, but in fact the root cause of the problem.

I can already hear your question: "What do you mean, pastor?"

Let me explain.

The most concerning thing about the church's condition isn't what has happened to the building or the furnishings—it's what has happened to the leaders and members, to their spirit. They've become so accustomed to their situation that they neither know, imagine, nor believe that they can change it. Do you see it?

The congregation's condition is not merely a symptom of a deeper issue; it is the issue itself. Why? There's a difference between saying "the church is sick" and saying "WE ARE a sick church." WE ARE a stagnant church. WE ARE a divided church. WE ARE a cold church. In the first instance, it's temporary. In the second, it's a matter of identity. Do you see the distinction?

Symptoms can change, but when a church identifies with its symptoms, it becomes the cause of them.

If I say, "the congregation is cold," I'm describing a symptom that can be changed. But if I say, "we are a cold congregation," I'm accepting that condition as something natural and unchangeable. It then becomes the condition, the cause, or the very nature of the congregation. It's like saying, "I have a headache" versus saying, "I am a headache." In the first case, we're discussing a temporary symptom; in the second, it's a permanent identity. Do we "have" a condition, or do we "become" it?

Understanding this is crucial because many churches have adopted their symptoms as part of their identity. At this point, the situation becomes even more alarming.

No matter how many opportunities the congregation has or how much the pastor and leaders want change, if the church isn't freed from the beliefs and practices that have held them back, any effort will be superficial, temporary, and ultimately fruitless.

Please read that last sentence again and reflect on it carefully. True leadership seeks a change in the church's identity. We must refuse to be known or defined by our shortcomings! We must clarify this from the outset: we cannot allow situations to take hold of us that could disappear if confronted with God's power. They must disappear!!

2. Let's acknowledge our mistaken beliefs to find liberation

Leadership begins in the mind. The leaders of this congregation wanted to grow—truly, they did! (Notice that I'm speaking in the past tense.) However, after many years of trying, they stopped believing. For them, the condition of the church had become bearable, even acceptable. Deep down, perhaps they thought that this, and nothing else, was "God's plan" for their congregation.

No matter what happened or which pastors came: they would remain the same! They might still carry the name of "church," but they weren't experiencing the promised power.

This condition reminds me of the message of the faithful witness to the church in Sardis[12], one of the seven churches in Asia Minor: " know your works, that you have a name that you are alive, but you are dead" (Revelation 3:1). They could still be called a congregation and have a building, but within, they lacked the power and life needed for growth and multiplication.

Have you ever heard a congregation's leaders say, "We've tried that before and it didn't work," "This church is different from the others," "That's just the way we are here," or "I've been around longer and I know this won't change"? Let me ask you: Is that church alive?

That's what I found as I walked through that place and looked around that fall. In my heart, I asked myself: Why am I here? Then God answered me: "This is why you're here!"

3. *Believe* that change is possible.

This "frozen condition," both physical and spiritual, can occur not only in small churches. I have also seen many large, well-established congregations, with decades of existence, that remain unchanged, frozen in time. The same leaders! The same members! They lack the vitality to grow themselves, let alone generate new churches. Often, the fruit of their efforts is minimal or even nonexistent. It's worth asking: Is this church sick? Has it aged? Is it dying?

The sick church: *It's not active.* A characteristic of a sick church is that a significant percentage of its members are not involved in spiritual, social, or missionary activities.

---

[12] Sardis, located about 80 kilometers east of Smyrna, was well known in the 6th century BC as the beautiful capital of Lydia. It was destroyed by an earthquake in AD 17 and later rebuilt under Tiberius. See Horst Balz and Gerhard Schneider, Exegetical Dictionary of the New Testament (Grand Rapids, MI: Eerdmans, 1990-), 229.

The aging church: *It's not productive.* Aging churches have lost their natural ability to reproduce. These congregations struggle to increase membership and even have difficulty establishing new churches.

The dying church: *It's losing members.* Dying congregations, in addition to being inactive and not reproducing, see a yearly decrease in membership.

What must we do to believe that change is possible? Although the situation may seem hopeless and our efforts in vain, if we understand and believe what God has promised, renewed life and power will flow into our ministry and congregation.

Read these five scriptures prayerfully and carefully, and reflect on the question: What is God's message to His leaders and people?

- "The parched ground *shall become* a pool, and the thirsty land springs of water; in the habitation of jackals, where each lay, there shall be grass with reeds and rushes." (Isaiah 35:7, emphasis added).
- "For I will *pour water* on him who is thirsty, and floods on the dry ground; I will pour my spirit on your descendants, and my blessing on your offspring;" (Isaiah 44:3, emphasis added).
- The wilderness and the wasteland shall be glad for them, and the desert *shall rejoice and blossom* as the rose; it shall blossom abundantly and rejoice, even with joy and singing. the glory of Lebanon shall be given to it, the excellence of Carmel and Sharon. they shall see the glory of the Lord, the excellency of our God." (Isaiah 35:1-2, emphasis added).
- "Until *the Spirit is poured upon us* from on high, and the wilderness becomes a fruitful field, and the fruitful field is counted as a forest" (Isaiah 32:15, emphasis added).

What is the image?

God sees His people in a state of spiritual drought during Isaiah's time. In the face of that barrenness, He promises to change their condition, transforming it from absence to the manifestation of His power.

What will happen?

The dryness and desolation will disappear, and in their place will arise pools, rivers, shelter, fertile fields, and forests. What a remarkable picture! These promises were given to a people suffering from the absence of God. The solution to their situation is clearly presented: water.

In these verses, water represents *the work of the Holy Spirit*, who will bring transformation to the people, just as water transforms a desert. No matter how dry and barren the desert is, it can be changed by the power of water.

A striking example is the Atacama Desert, one of the driest places on Earth. Yet, due to the weather phenomenon known as "El Niño," a miracle sometimes occurs: the desert blooms! Thanks to the rains, not only does greenery appear, but over 200 species of flowers burst into bloom. [13]

These biblical texts assure us that God has promised to change the situation of His people, no matter how desperate their condition may seem. He promises to transform the desert! Do you believe it? Does your church believe it? And most importantly, do your leaders believe it?

4. Put the solution into action

What do you need for the miracle of flourishing to occur in your congregation? The answer is the key to ending a ministry without results and to

---

[13]https://www.eluniversal.com.mx/destinos/el-extrano-fenomeno-que-hace-florecer-el-desierto.

reviving churches that are suffering from a lack of power and life. What's needed is water. Yes, water!

Imagine trying to revive a desert without water. It's like trying to drive a car without fuel. You can repaint it, install the most comfortable seats, and fill it with the most pleasant fragrance, but it won't move forward. It simply cannot run without energy. In the same way, the answer for a sick, aging, or dying church is the work of the Holy Spirit.

This process of spiritual renewal and flourishing is called revival. It *is the miracle God has planned for your congregation.* Do you believe it? Do your leaders believe it, too? God longs for each member and every church to become a fertile field—a forest for the glory of God!

Remember, revival is an ongoing process, and seeking the Holy Spirit is essential for maintaining spiritual vitality in any faith community. May God continue to bless your ministry!

This great and powerful truth can only be fully realized when we learn *not only to hear about God* but to hear God directly. He has a personal and specific message for each of our lives. Failing to understand this prevents the water of the Spirit from nourishing our hearts and those of the congregation.

What does this mean? Jesus explained it this way: "And when He comes, He will convict the world concerning sin, righteousness, and judgment" (John 16:8, ESV). It's not just about talking about water; it's about drinking it. It's not enough to know the truth if we're not *convicted* of our sinfulness. Water must be poured into our hearts and consciousness for us to experience its benefits—it cannot just touch our minds. Jesus understood this power when He said, "The Spirit gives life; the flesh counts for nothing. The words I have spoken to you are Spirit and they are life" (John 6:63, NIV). The only way to experience this life is to let the seed take deep root. Let it transform our minds! Then, we will be receiving the rain from heaven.

In this sense, let's always remember that hearing about God and hearing from God are two very different things. The Pharisees, Nicodemus, and Paul had all heard about God, but they had not yet heard His voice directly. That difference marks a significant change in our relationship with Him.

5. Revival begins within the church

I like the word "revival" because it implies more than just renewal or restoration; it means coming back to life, bringing even more life. And this aligns perfectly with what Christ promised: "I have come that they may have life, and that they *may have it more abundantly*" (John 10:10, ESV, emphasis added).

It is God's plan for His leaders and His people to experience life—life that is increasingly full and abundant. In this sense, there is no limit to the growth of life's power within the church. It can rise higher and higher. Revive your church! Revival breathes life into the dead and brings health to the sick.

Revival means experiencing the power of God. The goal of leaders is for their church to grow like the light of dawn, continually experiencing the fullness of the Holy Spirit's presence. Throughout history, God has used many individuals to bring about this revival.

Jonathan Edwards was a leading figure in the Great Awakening in North America.[14]When speaking about this revival, he stated that it was "God's primary means for the extension of his Kingdom."[15]For his part, revival historian Edwin Orr perceives them as "a movement of the Holy Spirit that produces a revival of New Testament Christianity in the Church of Christ and in the surrounding community."[16]

---

[14]Brian H. Edwards, *Revival: A people overflowing with God*, trans. Valerie Crespí-Green (Moral de Calatrava, Ciudad Real, Spain: Editorial Peregrino, 2001), 27.

[15]Edwards, *Revival: A people overflowing with God*, 27.

[16]Edwards, *Revival: A people overflowing with God*, 28.

Scottish evangelist Duncan Campbell, who participated in a 20th-century revival in the Hebrides, defines it as "a community overflowing with God."[17] Experiencing divine presence is the fundamental goal of true Christianity, and spiritual leaders must prioritize it in their congregations.

What is the result of the revival? Evan Roberts, a young man who for three years prayed for the revival in Wales that finally occurred after 1904, said: "My mission is first to the churches. When the churches awaken to duty, multitudes of men from the world will be introduced into the Kingdom. An entire church on its knees is irresistible."[18] However, this principle, which applies to the church as a whole, must first begin with the leader. A revived, prayerful leader is the first step toward reviving a church. This principle, attributed to Roberts, places the leader in a delicate position, as they become the divine spark that reignites spiritual life.

Why has revival not been achieved?

There are at least three key reasons why revival doesn't occur. Although the Spirit of God can convict us of this need and make us willing to obey, it's essential to understand the principles that make revival possible. As we explore each of these reasons, I invite you to set aside any barriers and walk the path that will lead us to the fulfillment of God's promise.

Revival is not the result of our efforts, but the product of God's work.

The first reason revival doesn't happen is because we often think it depends on us, rather than being a work of God. This mindset leads us to rely more on our own efforts and plans than on prayer and dependence on God. Remember

---

[17] Edwards, *Revival: A people overflowing with God*, 28.

[18] Edwards, *Revival: A people overflowing with God*, 29-30.

what the Scripture says: "Will you not revive us again, that your people may rejoice in you?" (Psalm 85:6 ESV). Life is a divine gift. Therefore, we must pray and depend on God more than ever to experience His work in us.

Revival is not the result of programs, but of love.

The second reason revival doesn't manifest is when ceremonies and rituals take priority over brotherly love and deep relationships among believers. Jealousy, gossip, and conflict can severely damage the spiritual life of a congregation. To sincerely seek revival, we must allow God's love to flood our lives.

Revival does not occur when there is a lack of trust.

The third reason congregations do not experience revival is when there is a lack of trust between members and their leaders. This mistrust can neutralize the influence and leadership needed for transformation. Pastors, elders, and church leaders must remember that it is not the position that grants the authority to create revival—it is the presence of the Holy Spirit in the leader.

6. The spirit of the leader the most important thing: the leader's spirit.

There are two fundamental truth that, when lived through the work of the Holy Spirit in the leader's heart, will empower them to fulfill their mission. This experience itself is the spark that can ignite revival. It is difficult, if not impossible, for a congregation to experience revival or reformation without this first spark in the leader's spirit.

The history of leaders such as Luther, Wesley, Moody, Spurgeon, Miller, Edwards, and others is a testament to this truth. They were the spark that ignited a spiritual fire. What they experienced is not exclusive to them—absolutely not!

You, dear reader, I, and *anyone willing can* experience the baptism of the Holy Spirit in our lives, enabling us to fulfill the mission God has entrusted to us.[19]

While this topic deserves a deeper conversation, allow me to highlight two actions that are essential for the Holy Spirit to work in the leader's spirit.

Prostrate Before the Cross

The Cross is the starting point. Without experiencing it, it's impossible to fully receive divine grace. Bowing before the cross means recognizing and reliving what Christ did for us on Calvary to free us from our sins. Before the cross, the Holy Spirit convicts us of "sin, righteousness, and judgment," and we experience divine forgiveness.

The leader must strip away their ego and be clothed in the power of divine forgiveness. Only God knows the human heart, and the conviction of sin in the leader's heart—whether public or internal—is the essential first step to experiencing the kingdom of God within their congregation. From this conviction comes confession. By aligning ourselves with God's perfect will, we recognize our faults and change our attitude toward them. Asking for God's forgiveness is the crucial step that sparks revival in the congregation. The Bible calls this repentance.

This understanding is vital. All growth in the kingdom of God within the church begins in the leader's heart. This process involves dying with Christ on

---

[19] Jesus said: "And I tell you, ask, and it will be given to you; seek, and you will find; knock, and it will be opened to you. For everyone who asks receives, and the one who seeks finds, and to the one who knocks it will be opened. What father among you, if his son asks for a fish, will instead of a fish give him a serpent; or if he asks for an egg, will give him a scorpion? If you then, who are evil, know how to give good gifts to your children, how much more will the heavenly Father give the Holy Spirit to those who ask him!" (Luke 11:9-13 ESV).

the cross, crucifying the old self and flesh, and allowing the Spirit of God to guide us (Galatians 2:20). Paul declared that he was crucified with Christ, and this experience *gave him power* in his ministry.

What is the result of Christ's victory on the Cross applied to our lives? The leader, empowered by this victory, gains the authority to confront Satan, the prince of this world, and intercede for God's promises in the lives of the congregation "in the name of Christ."

To be an instrument of blessing, we must humble ourselves at the foot of Calvary, surrender at the cross, and allow the presence of Christ—His power and authority—to fill us. Without this experience, we will not feel equipped to confront Satan and defeat him. The cross of Christ becomes the platform from which we can claim the promises and victories God has intended for our lives, our churches, and our congregations.

Everything—absolutely everything—can be gained, received, or accomplished through what Christ did for us on the cross of Calvary. It is there, and only there, that the kingdom of salvation and power is sustained. When the leader internalizes this experience of faith and recognizes the possession of this kingdom in their heart, they will be able to walk in it and work for the expansion of the kingdom through the power of the Holy Spirit.

This unique spiritual experience is what Christ emphasized to His disciples when He said, "I am the vine; you are the branches. Whoever abides in me and I in him, he it is that bears much fruit, for apart from me you can do nothing" (John 15:5, ESV). Abiding in Christ is essential for salvation and life in Him. Christ promises that those who experience this unity—whether members, leaders, families, or churches—will see abundant results. Life, fertile fields, and forests will be the outcomes of this real unity, the key to revival and transformation.

To summarize, the leader before the cross of Calvary must:

- Recognize their faults and ask for forgiveness.

- Accept their Savior and their new status as a redeemed child and participant in the kingdom of God.
- Understand that Satan cannot accuse them because their sins have been forgiven in Christ.

It is impossible for a leader to experience the fruits of revival in their church, among their members, or in the growth of God's kingdom without first standing at the foot of the cross and receiving the kingdom of God through the Holy Spirit.

However, once the leader has embraced their identity as a forgiven child of God, there is a second experience that must follow:

Sit on the Throne

We often emphasize the experience of the Cross when we talk about Christ—as if we must only be crucified with Him. But Scripture also highlights another vital aspect of the Christian experience: sitting on the throne!

Paul, in his letter to the Ephesians, writes: "and raised us up with him *and seated us with him in the heavenly places* in Christ Jesus" (Ephesians 2:6, ESV, emphasis added). Let me point out two important aspects of this text. First, the context. In the previous verse, Paul explains that through Christ's death, we have been given "life" when we are united with Him. Paul wrote: "even when we were dead in our trespasses, made us alive together with Christ—by grace you have been saved—" (Ephesians 2:5, ESV).

Immediately after describing our union with Christ on the cross, the text says: and God "raised us up" with Christ. Various translations affirm that this union with Christ not only brings salvation but also empowers us: we are "seated with Him in the heavenly places."

If every Christian understood and lived out this truth, more spiritual battles would be won, and the kingdom of God would be established on earth sooner.

Just as being on the cross signifies accepting forgiveness and salvation, sitting on the throne signifies accepting the authority and lordship of Christ.

When Christ sat down at the right hand of God, He also seated us there spiritually. Why? To give us spiritual authority in His kingdom.[20] The church today must delve into what this means—it's no different than what it meant in the past.

Peter emphasized this truth:

- "you also, as living stones, are being built up a spiritual house, a *holy priesthood*, to offer up spiritual sacrifices acceptable to God *through Jesus Christ.*" (1 Peter 2:5, emphasis added).

John, in the book of Revelation, wrote:

- "And from Jesus Christ, the faithful witness, the firstborn from the dead, and the ruler over the kings of the earth. To Him who loved us and washed us from our sins in His own blood, and *has made us kings and priests* to His God and Father, to Him be glory and dominion forever and ever. Amen" (Revelation 1:5-6, emphasis added).
- "And they sang a new song, saying: "You are worthy to take the scroll, and to open its seals; for You were slain, and have redeemed us to God by Your blood out of every tribe and tongue and people and nation, and *have made us kings and priests to our God*; and we shall reign on the earth." (Revelation 5:9-10, emphasis added).

For the New Testament church, Christ is King of Kings and Lord of Lords. This truth was the source of the disciples' authority on earth. They preached the gospel with the conviction that Christ had all authority in heaven and on earth

---

[20] Jesus said, "And I will give you the keys of the kingdom of heaven, and whatever you bind on earth will be bound in heaven, and whatever you loose on earth will be loosed in heaven." (Matthew 16:19).

Matthew 28:18). Therefore, when Peter entered the temple, he could authoritatively say to the paralyzed man: "In the name of Jesus Christ of Nazareth, rise up and walk" (Acts 3:6). And the man walked.

The New Testament shows us a church that prayed, and the kingdom of grace manifested in power. Every believer understood that they were part of Christ's body and kingdom on earth.

This spiritual authority enables believers to fight the good fight of faith and confront and overcome the principalities, powers, and "spiritual hosts of wickedness in the heavenly places" (Ephesians 6:12). Moses obtained victory over Amalek through authority and power in God. The story tells us that when he interceded in prayer, Joshua defeated the enemy. Is there a more powerful image to understand the power of prayer, which first secures victory in the heavenly places through Christ?

Sitting in the heavenly places with Christ means more than just being saved. It means we are joint heirs with Him—His authority is our authority, His power is our power, His mission is our mission. Just as those who follow the prince of the power of the air are empowered for his work, those who are in Christ experience His Spirit and power (Ephesians 2:2; 3:20).

Only prayer that claims the merits and authority of Christ in heaven will bring about God's kingdom on earth. Faith in Christ as Savior grants us forgiveness and salvation. Faith in Him as Lord gives us power and authority to be His instruments.

Moreover, our position in Christ assures us, by faith, that He fights every battle for us from His throne, confronting the powers of this world with His authority. Ultimately, it's not our battle but His. Just as He won our salvation on the cross, He wins our victories from His throne—for His glory.

7. Live in the kingdom of God.

By being a child of God, you can receive the abundant riches of His grace—everything the Father desires to give you because you are His child. This is your new identity in the kingdom! Luther, a Catholic monk, began to speak about God's grace and faith. His eyes were opened, allowing him to see beyond the structural and ceremonial, into the spiritual and divine. Yet, the ties remain; we need to understand that the kingdom of God is more than food and drink. When the Holy Spirit dwells in the heart, it manifests itself in:

God's Joy

The Christian who lives in the kingdom of God rejoices in the Lord. The world may offer struggles and trials, but being in Christ reveals a joy that is sustained by trust in God and His power (John 15:11; Luke 10:21; Galatians 5:22).

God's Love

Along with joy, it is essential to experience the true love of God in the heart of every believer. This is another spiritual experience that allows us to feel the kingdom of God (Galatians 5:14; Matthew 22:40; Romans 13:10). On the other hand, congregations that lack love do not truly know God and will not experience the reality of His kingdom (1 Corinthians 13:1-7).

God's Power

Paul said, "For the kingdom of God is not a matter of talk but of power" (1 Corinthians 4:20). Early Christians experienced the manifestation of God's kingdom in their lives and congregations. The book of Acts is a record that testifies to that power. Is it needed today? Many would say yes, but the real question is: Why don't we have it, and how can we experience it? This is a need that must be addressed in the hearts of believers.

God's Grace

Let's remember: through mercy, we don't receive what we deserve, and through grace, we receive what we do not deserve. When every believer is filled with grace, their heart is experiencing the fullness of God's presence. To extend grace as individuals and as a congregation is to experience Jesus, who came into the world "full of grace" (John 1:14).

God's Faith

Faith is one of the most important needs for both congregations and believers (Hebrews 11:6). In recent times, Christianity faces the challenge of increasing faith. Christ asked, "When the Son of Man comes, will He find faith on the earth?" (Luke 18:8). Today's Christian world is surrounded by materialism and humanistic thinking that excludes God and His power (Matthew 16:26-28). For a church that desires to experience the miracles of God, faith must grow. This journey is one that every Christian must learn to walk to strengthen their faith (Matthew 17:20; Revelation 14:12).

Divine Direction

The early church and Christians were guided by the Holy Spirit. They found their greatest joy in testifying of this reality (Acts 15:28-30). God directed the church, calling Paul and Barnabas to minister in Antioch and guiding Philip to meet the Ethiopian on the road to Gaza (Acts 8:29). Is God still manifesting His will to the church? Yes, but there is a growing need for divine direction in both congregations and individual believers. Every member needs to experience a personal relationship with God (Acts 7:13).

God's Provision

God has promised to meet the needs of His people. During His time on earth, Jesus demonstrated His ability to provide, even with limited resources. Today, many in the church long to see the fulfillment of God's promise that the righteous will not be forsaken and that He will provide for every need. This is a kingdom promise that must be experienced in every congregation.

Walking in the Spirit

Every Christian, especially leaders, is called to experience a deep relationship with the Holy Spirit and enjoy the fullness of God in their lives. Walking in the Spirit allows Christians to overcome the flesh and its desires (Galatians 5:24). It leads to a new level of freedom from sin, making us powerful instruments of God.

We are called to stop placing excessive emphasis on ceremonies as if they were sacraments, and instead seek to experience the power of God in our lives. By doing this, we reflect the life and character of God, as seen in Jesus. This is our goal.

Of course, we must remember that this experience is within our reach and is free. God is ready to pour out all these blessings from the unsearchable riches of His grace. Paul understood this when he wrote: "To me, who am less than the least of all the saints, this grace was given, that I should preach among the Gentiles the unsearchable riches of Christ" (Ephesians 3:8).

This is just the beginning. Leaders must embrace this vision of experiencing the power of God and share what they have seen, heard, and experienced with others. This is how grace and the kingdom of God work—they grow as they are shared.

Lead in the Spirit

When God called Zerubbabel, He gave him divine confirmation: "It is not by force nor by strength, but by my Spirit, says the Lord Almighty" (Zechariah 4:6, NLT). This statement holds as much power today as it did then. It remains the first and most important principle for witnessing change. Are you ready?

If you make this decision…

1. You will be prepared to fight this spiritual battle against supernatural powers, clothed in the armor of God.
2. You will surrender your life to God and allow the Holy Spirit to guide you in your own transformation and spiritual growth.
3. You will begin to pray and intercede fervently for the power of the Holy Spirit to be poured out in your life and in the life of the congregation, turning the desert into a fertile field.
4. You will join the army of intercessory leaders and members, crying out in the mornings for the conversion of hearts and the manifestation of God's kingdom in every member and in the congregation.
5. You will intercede like Moses, praying for deliverance and strength for the people to achieve victory over Satan.

Signature: _____ Date: _____

I am happy that you have reached this point in our study of leadership. How do you feel? What aspects have impacted your understanding of the leadership that God has entrusted to you today? Do you feel your faith growing as you contemplate how God can use you, just as His Word promises, to witness His power and glory?

These questions are important for reflection, to affirm the truths that need to take root in your understanding. After all, what's the point of reading if we forget what we've studied? You are welcome! That's why it's crucial to take time to pray, meditate, and decide how these teachings can find application in your life and ministry today. Think about everything that could happen. Just imagining it makes me excited about the effort that went into bringing this material to your hands... and it makes me dream of all that God will do through you. I believe it! Amen.

When you consider it appropriate, then let's go together to discover the true secret of growth in the next chapter.

3

The heart of the leader: THE SECRET TO GROWTH

Sitting in the turquoise chairs, we listened to the report. I looked around; we were all silent. The same thing had happened in previous years. "If we add all those who joined the congregation and subtract those who were disaffiliated, the result is..." The secretary paused and sighed, "fewer members than last year." Then he announced our current membership count.

Why do so many congregations experience this situation? Many people are added through baptism, yet by the end of each year, we have roughly the same number of members—or, in the worst case, fewer—often due to the passing of former members.[21]

When evaluating the stagnation or decline of congregations, it's almost certain that we'll come to the conclusion that we need to find a genuine strategy

---

[21]If we think about this carefully and compare it with the mission of preaching to the whole world, we will feel frustrated, worried, and even ashamed of the results of our efforts and leadership. The prophet Zechariah made it known: "But they refused to pay attention, and turned a stubborn shoulder and plugged their ears from hearing. They also made their hearts as hard as a diamond so that they could not hear the Law and the words which the Lord of armies had sent by His Spirit through the former prophets; therefore great wrath came from the Lord of armies." (Zechariah 7:11-12).

to change this reality. What are we striving for? The answer is obvious: to have more people next year!

In all my years of ministry, I saw many leaders, pastors, and congregations deeply concerned about real membership growth. It's painful to admit that their efforts, like mine, often felt futile. "We need to redefine success" was a common phrase from a colleague who designed new slogans and strategies every year. It was exhausting—new meetings, improved strategies, training sessions, and motivational talks.

Fortunately, at some point, I discovered the reason why every year I found myself starting over from the same place. Is this how the early church operated? I didn't think so, and I imagine you'd agree.[22]

I finally gathered the courage to make the second decision that changed my ministry. My dear reader, I want you to consider that if this decision is not made, we will remain like airplanes in cruising flight—maintaining the same altitude—when we dream of reaching the stars.

I insist: after visiting dozens of congregations across North, Central, and South America, I've observed that this problem, or reality, is a recurring issue in a significant percentage of churches. To reverse this trend, various options for consolidating and growing membership have been explored, ranging from enhancing the quality of new members through more thorough pre-baptism training to intensifying follow-up care by hosting different types of events, such as trainings, worship services, and social activities. In summary, emotional support and cognitive growth are usually the two main objectives in church programs. Yet, the goal remains elusive.

---

[22]According to the pastoriad.org page, only 21.8% of congregations had a growth in active membership between 2023 and 2024. 64.8% remained with the same number of members and 13.4% decreased. However, the percentage of congregations with declining membership is increasing as postmodernism and secularism grow in society.

So, let's return to the essential question: How can we carry out our pastoral ministry in a way that truly leads to church growth? I've come to believe that in order to increase growth and reduce membership attrition, we must have a deeper understanding of what it truly means to shepherd. Among other things, this is the next crucial step in transforming your congregation.

What does it mean to shepherd, watch over, and nurture?

There are two Greek words that arise from the message of Paul (Acts 20:28) and Peter (1 Peter 5:1-3), which allow us to clearly see the concept of shepherding. The first term is used by Paul in his message in Miletus to the elders of Ephesus: "Be on guard." The word "be on guard" comes from the Greek word *prosejo*, which means pay attention, be concerned. We can see the particular emphasis of the elders' special concern for the members of the church. If we stop to analyze the way Paul wrote the term "be on guard", we will not realize that it is in the imperative verbal mood, which expresses orders or exhortations for the completion of the action.

For his part, Peter, in his first universal epistle uses the term *poimaino*, which was translated as "shepherd" and which means to take care of the flock. Finally, the Manual of the Seventh-day Adventist Church states: "as sub-pastors, the elders must constantly watch over the flock."[23]

Pastoral work involves a deep concern, interest, and commitment to the well-being and care of God's flock. Now, the following questions arise: Is the pastoral ministry of elders truly understood and practiced? Do the elders show a genuine interest in the flock? Do the elders know those whom they have been called to shepherd? Are the elders fulfilling their biblical responsibility to care

---

[23] Seventh-day Adventist Manual Church - 2022 Edition (Doral, FL: IADPA, 2022), 73.

for the flock? What is said about the pastoral role of elders?[24] In relation to the responsibility of elders, the Church Manual provides two important statements that help us understand the elder's pastoral role. The first statement says: "The pastor is not to concentrate all responsibilities on himself, but rather share them with the elders and other church leaders."[25] It is clear that the responsibility of shepherding is shared with the elders, who act as undershepherds of God's flock.

The second statement reaffirms this idea:

"The pastoral work of the church must be shared by the pastor and the elders. The elders, in common agreement with the pastor, must visit church

---

[24]"Paul also considered elders to be a vital function of the early church; In particular, he asks his colleague Titus to appoint elders in each city of Crete (Titus 1:7). In both Acts and Paul's letter to Titus, the term "elder" and the term "overseer" (also translated as "bishop") are essentially synonymous (Acts 20:28 refers to "overseers" as "overseers"). elders" in Acts 20:17 and Titus 1:5-9). This is the group of people that oversees the operations of the church. This is the closest thing to a clear hierarchy that we see in the early church... 1 Timothy 4:14 refers to a group of elders as the "council of elders" (πρεσβυτέριον, presbyterion), apparently indicating an organized administrative body.

"If one accepts the view that Paul had the offices of the church in mind, then it can also be argued that these offices were types of elders. This does not suggest that the people in those positions in the church were the only elders, but rather that if a person held a position in the church they were a de facto elder and/or that people with particular positions in the church were selected from among the elders. church...

"In the early church, elders offered spiritual guidance and supervision. Paul provides the qualifications for elders in 1 Timothy 3:1-7 and Titus 1:5-9 (compare Acts 14:23; 1 Peter 5:1-4)." John D. Barry, "Early Church Governance," Lexham Bible Dictionary, ed. John D. Barry and Lazarus Wentz (Bellingham, WA: Lexham Press, 2014).

[25] Church Manual, 73.

members, care for the sick, encourage the ministry of prayer, lead or officiate at the ceremony of anointing the sick and the dedication of children, encourage the discouraged, and participate in other pastoral responsibilities.".[26]

It is noteworthy how this statement clearly outlines some of the responsibilities that church leaders must carry out:

1.   Visit members.

2.   Assist the sick.

3.   Invite each member to engage in prayer.

4.   Anoint the sick.

5.   Dedicate children.

6.   Encourage the discouraged.

7.   Fulfill other pastoral duties related to the comprehensive care of members.

What the Church Manual presents is in harmony with the pastoral work of the early church leaders, who made a constant effort to meet the needs of the members and strengthen them through preaching in the temple and tireless house-to-house visitation.[27]

Ellen White adds insight into the spirit a leader should embody when fulfilling these pastoral duties:

Those who occupy the position of *undershepherds* are to exercise a watchful diligence over the Lord's flock. This is not to be a dictatorial

---

[26]Church Manual, 73.

[27]The apostles were dedicated to ensuring that the needs of all congregations were met. Offerings were collected and promoted as part of the church's stewardship. Additionally, as the apostle Paul demonstrates, members were visited in their homes, and letters were written to encourage them in their faith and to assess their spiritual condition (Acts 2:45, 4:32, 20:31 and 1 Corinthians 16: 13).

vigilance, but one that tends to encourage and strengthen and uplift. Ministry means more than sermonizing; it means earnest, personal labor. The church on earth is composed of erring men and women, who need patient, painstaking effort that they may be trained and disciplined to work with acceptance in this life, and in the future life to be crowned with glory and immortality. Pastors are needed— faithful shepherds—who will not flatter God's people, nor treat them harshly, but who will feed them with the bread of life—men who in their lives feel daily the converting power of the Holy Spirit and who cherish a strong, unselfish love toward those for whom they labor.[28]

When elders and leaders are not prepared to assume the responsibilities of shepherding the congregation—caring for it individually and with love—the church suffers.

In this regard, congregations must pray and seek leaders who will serve God by shepherding the church according to His revealed will. This process requires that, like Samuel, we not be impressed by the first, second, or subsequent candidates, but wait until we find the right one—the one God has prepared for the task.

Ellen White declared:

In some of our churches the work of organizing and of ordaining elders has been premature; the Bible rule has been disregarded, and consequently grievous trouble has been brought upon the church. There should not be so great haste in electing leaders as to ordain men who are in no way fitted for the responsible work—men who need to

---

[28]Ellen G. White, The Acts of the Apostles (Doral, FL: IADPA, 2006), 526, emphasis added.

be converted, elevated, ennobled, and refined before they can serve the cause of God in any capacity.[29]

He also adds:

There is tactful work for the undershepherd to do as he is called to meet alienation, bitterness, envy, and jealousy in the church, and he will need to labor in the spirit of Christ to set things in order. Faithful warnings are to be given, sins rebuked, wrongs made right, not only by the minister's work in the pulpit, but by personal labor. The wayward heart may take exception to the message, and the servant of God may be misjudged and criticized. Let him then remember that "the wisdom that is from above is first pure, then peaceable, gentle, and easy to be entreated, full of mercy and good fruits, without partiality, and without hypocrisy. And the fruit of righteousness is sown in peace of them that make peace. James 3:17-18.[30]

Do we feed the flock according to God's heart?

As a leader, this question takes you beyond the abstract, intellectual, and theoretical aspects of leadership. What does it mean? It emphasizes that the vision and purpose we pursue as leaders must align with God's objective. This alignment will have a profound impact and ensure the success of God's plan in the lives of church members.

When we examine the divine example left by Christ, we gain a clearer understanding of the fundamental nature of mission. He confirms that He "came to seek and to save the lost" (Luke 19:10; Matthew 18:11). This redemptive perspective underscores the salvific focus of His mission. His work

---

[29]Ellen G. White, Testimonios, Tomo 5, p. 617.2

[30]White, The Acts of the Apostles, 526.

was not a celebratory cruise on a paradisiacal beach, but a rescue mission for those shipwrecked.

Additionally, we see that Christ's primary purpose in shepherding was directed toward those in need of a shepherd. In the parable of the lost sheep, the shepherd "leaves" the ninety-nine and goes out to search for the one that was "lost" (Luke 15:4). To emphasize this focus, Jesus stated: "It is not the healthy who need a doctor, but the sick" (Matthew 9:12). The logical question then is: Who needs a pastor? The answer: those who have strayed from the path, the sick sheep who cannot follow the shepherd!

Do you understand the value of 'one'?

In summary, when we examine Jesus and His ministry, we see two key emphases:

1.   The worth of one individual to heaven.

2.   The priority of heaven.

The power of Christ's leadership lay in the fact that it was not centered on strategy, events, or programs, but on people. I hope many images come to mind of moments when Christ stopped to meet a need. This model, and no other, should be adopted by leaders and members who seek to resolve the church's challenges and witness unprecedented growth. Valuing the individual is essential.

When leaders focus on programs rather than people, the kingdom of God does not grow in the hearts of the members but instead loses its power with each passing day. Let's take a moment to reflect on the characteristics of these two types of ministry.

Program-Focused	Member-Centered
Most of the time is spent organizing programs.	Most of the time is spent visiting and serving members.
A large percentage of resources is allocated to carrying out activities.	The largest percentage of resources is dedicated to meeting the needs of the members.
Leaders are often unaware of the exact number of members they should be serving, who is attending church, who is sick, or the spiritual condition of the members.	Leaders know exactly how many members are in their church, who attends regularly, who is sick, and the spiritual condition of each member.
Members respect the leader for his position and leadership.	Members love the leader and follow him in response to his genuine love and care for them.

To improve the effectiveness of ministry, we need to see each church member as a soul we must guide to salvation, disciple, and help mature—not merely as a spectator of our meetings or a statistic. Jesus died on the cross of Calvary for every person. And for just one of them, Christ would have given His life. A Christian leader who is committed to following Christ's example will value every person in their ministry.

The leader in front of me paused as he spoke. I think I understood why. He cared about me and didn't want to hurt my heart as a young pastor. "The problem isn't deciding to baptize them, pastor. The problem is that in just a short time, weeks or months, they will stop attending." His eyes filled with emotion. In that moment, I realized it wasn't just about sparing my feelings— he carried a deep pain in his heart. He didn't want to experience the joy of seeing his church grow, only to face the despair of watching members leave. He continued, "It's better to wait a little while to see if their decision to serve God is driven only by emotion." Then he sat down. I looked at the nodding faces of several congregation members.

That night, I understood the need to find a solution to the issue of growth and attrition. They valued each person and worked hard to win them over, wanting them to stay in the congregation. Could I think any differently?

This experience, like a seed, took root in my heart. It grew until I realized that if I could value each member as Jesus did, not only would people join and remain, but I could mobilize multitudes.

Can you see it too? Growth, retention, and mobilizing crowds.

As for mobilizing crowds, this material doesn't cover that in depth—more of that is discussed in my book *Let's Dream Big: Leadership That Makes the Difference*. However, consider the impact Christ's ministry had on people. No one was invisible to Him. He called people down from trees, asked for water, noticed when someone touched Him in a crowd, and healed a paralyzed man who had waited for years for someone to bring him to the pool at the right moment. Do you see it? No leader can lead multitudes without first valuing the individual. We can't have 100 sheep if we lose ONE!

Leaders who grow: understand the priority of heaven

If the priority of heaven, according to Jesus, is the care of the sheep, then shepherds of all times must accept the call to faithfully fulfill this task. In this sense, elders must address the following practical aspects of caring for the flock that God has entrusted to them.

Do you truly care for the members under your responsibility? As leaders, we must understand that He, and only He, is responsible for the number of members in His flock.[31] Furthermore, when discussing pastoral work in relation to the

---

[31] One of the most important aspects of pastoral work is knowing the exact number of members we must care for. Even true shepherds know everything about

members or "sheep" of the fold, Scripture makes it clear that the pastor must give special attention to those with spiritual needs. They should be at the center of pastoral care.

At first, this wasn't very clear to me. Perhaps I wasn't inclined to embrace this task, or maybe I was too focused on preparing and leading various events. Somehow, I didn't realize that this was my primary responsibility. My perspective began to shift when I baptized 14 people in a congregation that had been unable to organize as a church for more than 18 years. Now, I couldn't— and didn't want to—lose a single member. That moment marked the beginning of exponential growth in a district that expanded to eight congregations in just over two years. Yes, two years!

I am firmly convinced that God desires His kingdom to grow without limits, according to His perspective: He is not willing to lose anyone. That may happen, but it is not His purpose. Jesus said, "While I was with them, I kept them in your name… none of them is lost except the son of perdition, that the Scripture might be fulfilled" (John 17:12, emphasis added).

At this point, you might be wondering what you need to do to effectively shepherd and retain your congregation. I found the answer clearly laid out in the book of Ezekiel. The text says:

> You have *not strengthened* the weak or *healed* the sick or *bound up* the injured. You have not *brought back* the strays or *searched for* the lost. You have ruled them harshly and brutally. So they were scattered because there was no shepherd, and when they were scattered they became food for all the wild animals. My sheep wandered over all the mountains and on every high hill. They were scattered over the whole

---

their flock, their average age, gender, challenges, work, dreams, direction, and more. The list is endless. But it is the job of the true shepherd to fully know his flock.

earth, and no one searched or looked for them." (Ezekiel 34:4-6,NIV, emphasis added).

I believe this passage is one of the most powerful references to pastoral work. However, its content hasn't received the necessary attention in the training of pastors, nor in the evaluation of ministerial work.

Now, dear leader, the meaning of this passage becomes clearer when you understand its context. The people of Israel had not listened to their prophets. Instead, their kings, priests, "prophets," and leaders had chosen to follow their own plans to protect the nation from Babylonian attack. The result was captivity. The prophet Ezekiel, already in captivity, under God's inspiration, pointed out that the leaders' priority was to care for themselves rather than tending to God's flock:

> Son of man, prophesy against the shepherds of Israel; prophesy and say to them: 'This is what the Sovereign Lord says: Woe to you shepherds of Israel who only take care of yourselves! Should not shepherds take care of the flock? ³ You eat the curds, clothe yourselves with the wool and slaughter the choice animals, but *you do not take care of the flock.* (Ezekiel 34:2-3,NIV, emphasis added).

What was the result of such negligence? "My sheep wandered over all the mountains and on every high hill. They *were scattered* over the whole earth, and *no one searched or looked for them*" (Ezekiel 34:6, NIV; emphasis added).

These texts reveal the depth of God's love for His church. They clearly show that the condition of the people is often the result of the actions of their leaders.

God's response to this situation is clear, highlighting both the seriousness of the leaders' actions and His own faithfulness:

> Therefore, *you shepherds, hear the word of the Lord*: as surely as I live, declares the Sovereign Lord, because my flock lacks a shepherd and so *has been plundered* and has become food for all the wild animals, and

because *my shepherds did not search for my flock* but *cared for themselves rather than for my flock,* therefore, you shepherds, hear the word of the Lord: This is what the Sovereign Lord says: I am against the shepherds and *will hold them accountable for my flock.* I will *remove them from tending the flock so that the shepherds can no longer feed themselves. I will rescue my flock from their mouths, and it will no longer be food for them.* "For this is what the Sovereign Lord says: *I myself will search for my sheep and look after them.* As a shepherd looks after his scattered flock when he is with them, so will I look after my sheep. *I will rescue them from all the places where they were scattered* on a day of clouds and darkness. I will bring them out from the nations and gather them from the countries, and I will bring them into their own land. I will pasture them on the mountains of Israel, in the ravines and in all the settlements in the land. I will tend them in a good pasture, and the mountain heights of Israel will be their grazing land. *There they will lie down in good grazing land, and there they will feed in a rich pasture on the mountains of Israel.* I myself will tend my sheep and have them lie down, declares the Sovereign Lord. I will search for the lost and bring back the strays. I will bind up the injured and strengthen the weak, but the sleek and the strong I will destroy. I will shepherd the flock with justice. (Ezekiel 34:7-16, NIV, emphasis added).

Don't you think these words are enough to help us understand the depth of the message for leaders today? Reading, reflecting, and writing about this passage always warms my heart. It causes me to evaluate how well I am fulfilling the task of shepherding. After all, it's not about pleasing men but about pleasing God, who, as the apostle Paul says, "considered me faithful, appointing me to His service" (1 Timothy 1:12).

Consequently, the Holy Spirit must examine our hearts and help us see, according to our conscience, how well we are meeting God's expectations in caring for His flock. Take time for reflection. And if necessary, kneel and pray to God, just as I did.

Seeking Pastors After God's Own Heart

The absence of appropriate pastoral leadership that addresses the ruinous condition of the flock compels God to seek shepherds after His own heart. This was the message of the prophet Jeremiah, who was in Jerusalem while Ezekiel was in Babylon (Jeremiah 3:15).

It is not God's plan for His flock to lack pastoral attention and care. God expects shepherds to watch over the flock and its condition! This is why the shepherd in Christ's parable, upon realizing that one sheep was missing, concentrated all his effort on searching for it (Luke 15:1-7). This is a shepherd after God's own heart!

What is the responsibility of the shepherd of the flock should do? Let us continue examining Ezekiel's message to the pastors or leaders of that time. The prophet speaks of weak, sick, injured, strayed, and lost sheep. These five conditions reveal the different levels of physical and spiritual needs within the flock. Each of these needs must be identified and ministered to by church leaders, in cooperation with the pastor.

Strengthen the weak sheep

In the first case, weak sheep may be physically or spiritually diminished. These sheep cannot walk long distances, they remain seated, and they always lag behind as the flock moves forward. You might ask: Pastor, what does this condition of weakness mean for the flock in my church? I suggest that these sheep may represent members who arrive late to church and have little participation in services and ministries.

The pastor needs to strengthen the faith of these members through the nourishment of God's Word. Additionally, we must pray for the Holy Spirit to affirm His convictions in their hearts and enable them to fulfill both His will and actions (Philippians 2:13). One of the important aspects is to invite them to experience the Lordship of Christ. God as King and Lord of their lives must become the most important experience in their spiritual journey.

Cure Sick Sheep

Sick sheep cannot move; they need help to do so. They are like the paralytic who had to be carried by four friends into Christ's presence (Mark 2:14-16). Without that great effort, the sick man would never have reached Jesus. These sheep may represent members who rarely attend church. These symptoms show that they are spiritually ill. What should local church leaders do?

The shepherd's goal is to prevent the illness from destroying the sheep. Whether the illness is physical or spiritual, the leader must give their full attention to discovering the real cause that leads the sheep away from God. The leader acts like a doctor, diagnosing what is affecting their spiritual life. The medicine must come from God's Word, and the strength to apply it comes through prayer.

In such cases, it's important to invite them to experience the guidance of the Holy Spirit, who is revealed in the most holy place. It is God's power that will guide each person to understand what needs attention. The promise is that the Spirit will guide us into all truth, showing us the way (John 16:8).

Bandage Injured Sheep

These sheep can walk, but not very well. Each step is painful because something has affected their mobility. Time may help, but unless treated properly, they can suffer long-term effects.

Who are the injured sheep in our congregation? There may be many answers, but let me suggest a few. These are sheep who have made mistakes or have suffered external circumstances, such as divorce, whether by personal decision or the actions of others. In both cases, they are wounded spiritually,

No more frustrated leaders and lifeless churches

which prevents them from moving forward as they once did. Shepherds and elders must care for these sheep to avoid spiritual illness or even death.

These sheep need to experience Christ's forgiveness, which was made possible on the sacrificial altar. They must believe and experience the healing of Christ's blood in their lives, so that their sins and mistakes can be covered by His righteousness (Isaiah 61:10). Repentance and faith are the path to restoration.

Bring back the stray sheep

Lost sheep are not with the flock; they are far from it. These sheep represent those who have drifted away from the church but whose names are still on the membership roll.

Being away from church doesn't mean being outside the church. For these sheep, leaders must remind them of their covenant with God made in the washing of water. They need the opportunity to renew their relationship with God by accepting the grace of Christ in their lives and trusting that the One who began a good work in them will bring it to completion (Philippians 1:6). What a great promise!

Search for the Lost Sheep

At the end of the day, we don't know where these sheep are. The flock has been gathered and counted, but the whereabouts of some sheep remain unknown. These could represent those whose names no longer appear on the church membership list. Yet, it's remarkable that God continues to seek them and expects His shepherds to keep those sheep in mind, even those considered "lost." Shepherds after God's heart are invited to reach out and attempt to change the condition of these sheep, even when recovery seems unlikely.

God does not strengthen, heal, or bring back these sheep, but He seeks them. The work in their hearts belongs to God, but it is the pastor's responsibility to ensure that they know we are there for them. This image reminds me of what God did with our first parents, Adam and Eve. Though they hid, God sought them—not to shame them, but to support them and bless them with garments to cover their nakedness.

The Lord Jesus came to seek His own in order to bless them, not to condemn but to save. And this act of being there for those who, by their own decisions, are no longer part of the flock is what will distinguish a ministry after God's heart. Jesus said:

> That you may be sons of your Father in heaven; for He makes His sun rise on the evil and on the good, and sends rain on the just and on the unjust. For if you love those who love you, what reward have you? Do not even the tax collectors do the same? And if you greet your brethren only, what do you do more than others? Do not even the tax collectors do so? Therefore you shall be perfect, just as your Father in heaven is perfect. (Matthew 5:45-48).

Salvation is a complete fact and, furthermore, a permanent process.[32]This is what Paul spoke of when he said that he who began the work will finish it (Philippians 1:6). This is why leaders must understand that baptism is not the end of the work entrusted by God, but rather the beginning of the task.

Jesus himself gave an example of how the leader should get involved and how to do this task of perfecting the saints. How Christ carried out this discipleship was presented in the book *Leadership that Transforms*. We need to understand what transforming grace means in our lives through the work of the Holy Spirit.

It is through the power of the Holy Spirit that every Christian can attain the stature of Christ. Jesus envisioned growth through discipleship when He stated the Great Commission: "teaching them to observe all things that I have

---

[32]The Bible refers to this; it calls it justification and sanctification.

commanded you" (Matthew 28:20). This is the goal and task of the leader: to shepherd the flock according to the pattern of Christ and the heart of God.

The value of one, as a priority for the Christian leader

When, as a leader, you have a sincere desire to understand the secrets of growth in your congregation, it is essential to apply the value of each individual to your leadership and to those who work alongside you. Jesus himself powerfully demonstrated this truth in His ministry when He declared, "None have been lost." The Master's main purpose was the salvation of all those under His care. Should it be any different for us?

I am convinced that, as in the parable, we will never achieve 100 sheep if we don't value each ONE and dedicate all our effort to finding the lost ONE. And, if we take this concept to its ultimate conclusion, we won't reach 101, 102, and beyond without recognizing the worth of each individual. Do you see it?

When I share this seminar, I cannot overlook how Jeremiah—a contemporary of Ezekiel—posed a crucial question to the leaders of his time, who had neglected God's guidance and failed to protect the people. This question remains relevant and even more pressing today. How will we respond to our responsibility as leaders: "Where is the flock that I gave you?"

Allow me to make this practical. The question asks: Where are those who joined your congregation five years ago, last year, or this year? Where are the youth, children, or adults who were once baptized? Can we answer this question? And, most importantly, does this question occupy a central place in the evaluation of our church's strategic actions and leadership? In other words, are the departments and activities we organize aligned to answer this question with integrity? As Christ affirmed: "None of those You gave me is lost."

I confess that this question stirs me deeply. Each time I reflect on it, I consider it in terms of my family, my church, and the leaders under my responsibility. The responsibility feels overwhelming because this is not just about being accountable to ourselves, our peers, or our organization, but to God Himself, who GAVE us the flock to care for.

What should we do?

Ellen White stated: "Personal interest and vigilant, individual effort will accomplish more for the cause of Christ than can be wrought by sermons or creeds".[33] This statement shifts our focus to where it truly belongs: the person! The one! The individual! Such effort will be more rewarding than regular preaching or teaching: personal attention and individual effort.

In other words, the strategy needed to achieve this objective requires an organizational approach centered on the individual, aiming to apply what Solomon already expressed: "Be diligent *to know the state* of your flocks, *And* attend to your herds" (Proverbs 27:23, emphasis added).

As I mentioned before, one of my districts consisted of congregations that had only held group status for 18 years. The reason was that those who had been baptized would eventually leave the congregation. So, when I baptized the first 14 people at the close of my campaign, I was determined to care for these new members as if they were my greatest treasure. For the church to grow, they had to remain.

One Saturday morning, as part of my usual routine, I checked to ensure that everyone who had been baptized was present—I would "count the flock." That day, I asked someone to do it for me while I prepared for the worship service. Before the service began, I received the report: A couple was missing. Since we didn't have cell phones back then, and I didn't know what had happened, I told the first elder they would have to wait for me to start the service until I returned because I was going to visit these members at their home.

---

[33]Review and Herald, September 6, 1881, emphasis added.

The head elder was surprised that I would adjust the timing of the sermon to go visit a single family. For him, the priority was the event; for me (perhaps in an extreme way), the priority was the sheep. How could I preach without knowing what had happened to them? Moreover, I wanted them to learn the importance of watching over the flock. I was a shepherd of the flock!

I will never forget that day. A brother gave me a ride, and I was able to minister to a family who needed affection, encouragement, and guidance to continue maturing in their faith. Most of all, they appreciated knowing that their pastor cared enough to visit and pray with them before preaching. That effort, and many others, was worth it. More than thirty years have passed, and these brothers remain faithful leaders in a congregation that has become prosperous and a great blessing.

I firmly believe that this experience represents the essence of personal interest and individual effort.

Personal interest and individual effort

How can we show personal interest and individual effort to each church member? After understanding what this ministry entails, it's essential to know how to implement it. You may be thinking about all the responsibilities you manage and the few people committed to helping. And if membership grows, how is it possible to continue with the same purpose and efficiency?

Each of these questions was answered for me when I understood the method Jethro taught Moses: Divide the congregation and assign people to care for them! (Exodus 18:1-25). This method established a structure focused on people.

Applying this principle at all levels—and especially as president of a union with over 800 congregations and 100,000 members—had an unprecedented impact. In *Dream Big, Lead, and Make a Difference*, you can find details on how God allowed the largest number of baptisms in the Inter-American Division to occur in one territory, and the establishment of 100 congregations in a single year in the third most populous city of the Inter-American Division.[34]

When we talk about implementing Moses' model, we should consider the following:

1. Assign a *group leader* for every 10 members.
2. Make a *church elder* responsible for 15 to 50 members, depending on the elder's location and experience.
3. Assign each elder one or two *deacons and deaconesses*. When an elder is responsible for more than 30 members, they should work with two deacons and two deaconesses to ensure pastoral care for that group.

Organizing the church in this way will allow for:

- *Efficiently serving* EVERY ONE of the congregation's members.
- Leading and *impacting* CROWDS.
- *Achieving goals* with EFFECTIVENESS.
- *Preventing* leader EXHAUSTION.

The leaders responsible for each member can fulfill their pastoral duties as follows:

1. Make a monthly visit to check on each member's spiritual, physical, and emotional state. Every member in their care should be visited monthly.
2. Take every opportunity to pray with members about their challenges, that God may strengthen their faith and reveal Himself in their lives.

---

[34] The Inter-American Division is an organization that serves 42 countries from Mexico to Colombia and Guyana.

3.   Provide support for food needs when necessary, as well as spiritual encouragement.

4.   Hold prayer meetings for members alongside small group leaders, deacons, deaconesses, and other church elders.

5.   Participate in weekly or biweekly meetings to pray together and report on the condition of the flock and the work being done.

Threats and obstacles

Implementation of the pastoral care plan for members is neither automatic nor without challenges. Quite the opposite. The church's program-centered rather than member-centered approach creates a steep and winding path to the desired change. This implementation requires a true paradigm shift among leaders and an unwavering commitment to a biblical worldview.

The obstacles I'll mention here are common, though not exclusive, and each can be addressed in multiple ways. I'll share some of the most effective alternatives.

3   *Numerous events demanding our attention.*

This obstacle is rooted in the organizational culture and represents one of the biggest challenges to implementing a biblical pastoral care program. The reason is simple: organizational culture can overshadow good strategies. If it isn't feasible to reduce the number of events, it's essential to introduce a new cultural action within the church setting. To successfully implement this change, we need to address the excess of events as part of the church's evaluation. This will reinforce a new identity and worldview for the congregation, paving the way for a cultural shift!

In Chapter 4, we'll explore how reducing or simplifying events can create space for a more personal and less formal church environment. To support implementation, additional actions will be highlighted and emphasized through ongoing evaluation.

3   *Taking time to prepare leaders and launch the plan.*

This obstacle is closely related to time management within the congregation. Here, leaders will need to prioritize what is essential for their ministry, understanding that achieving this will require sacrifice. Leaders must dedicate time to training seminars. Just as evaluation is essential to effect cultural change, training is crucial to transforming the leadership and church paradigm.

3   *Preference for what has always been done.*

This obstacle often relates to the character of leaders and the commitment of church members. An underlying cause may be a lack of spiritual depth and dedication to God. Here, the solution is to deepen our understanding that the path to change, success, or God's blessing is presented in Scripture as a narrow road of self-denial. Jesus clearly taught that self-denial involves "pruning" our desires to bear fruit. It's essential to lead leaders and members to reflect on their willingness to obey God: How committed are we? This kind of transformation can only come through prayer, studying the Word, and re-dedication to God in prayer weeks and retreats.

3   *Doubt, fear, and uncertainty.*

This obstacle is closely tied to the previous one and may be its deepest root. Leaders may fear that emphasizing certain changes could hinder productivity. I am convinced that this internal challenge—doubt or fear—is often due to a lack of faith. The answer is to revisit and meditate on the scriptures we have discussed. Remember, faith comes by hearing the Word of God. To overcome fear or doubt, it's crucial to recall that what we do is in obedience to God's Word.

3   *If others aren't doing it, why should I?*

Great revivals occurred when men and women, under God's conviction, chose to remain faithful to their conscience. Important questions to consider here are: Do I want to please God? Why not me? Does this go against any biblical principles or church practices? I am convinced that only individuals with a spirit like Luther's—rooted in the Word and guided by conscience—can lead the church to a new level in its relationship with God. Do you agree? If God has placed this conviction in your heart, I encourage you to take the next step. God will be with you. I believe it!

Evaluation

To close this chapter, here is an evaluation of how this principle is applied in your ministry and congregation.

Evaluation of the Church and Leaders in Implementing the Growth Plan:

1. Have leaders been trained in ministry after God's heart? Yes___ No___
2. Is the church membership list up to date? Yes___ No___
3. Have elders, deacons, deaconesses, small group, and department leaders received a list of the members they are responsible for? Yes___ No___
4. Are leaders visiting, praying with, and meeting the needs of their assigned members monthly? Yes___ No___
5. Are weekly or biweekly meetings held to pray, evaluate, plan, and recognize the elders, along with reports on members' well-being? Yes___ No___
6. Is the growth of active members in the congregation reviewed monthly at the church board and other meetings? Yes___ No___
7. Is there a budget for the church and small groups to meet members' needs? Yes___ No___

What's the next step to see God's work manifest in your ministry? I invite you to read the next chapter prayerfully and carefully. Take all the time you need to reflect while applying the principles you've already learned. Begin a training plan with your leaders using this material right away. It's time to share what God ias done for you and act in faith! In the next chapter, you will better understand he reason for taking this step.

4

The fighting scenario: THE SECRET OF VICTORY

His question was sincere: *How is it possible for us to build an entire healthy living center complex?* One of the members of the national church board expressed this genuine concern, and I had the same question. In a country with limited resources and materials, it seemed like a utopian dream, an impossibility.

Leading a church in a place where a pastor's salary barely equaled around twenty dollars, and where basic materials such as cement, iron, sandpaper, gasoline, and transportation parts were scarce, felt like a struggle between vision and reality. An annual inflation rate of 200%, coupled with food and medicine shortages, added further challenges. The project seemed like an illusion, a crazy endeavor. How could we achieve this goal when, even twenty-five years earlier, we hadn't managed to secure adequate land for construction?

Perhaps the reader has never experienced coordinating the actions of a national church amid unfavorable financial, social, political, and missionary circumstances. It's a monumental challenge. Leading anywhere is a challenge in itself, but in such a place, it could even be a risk.[35] I was required to represent

---

[35] There are many situations or experiences that require prudent silence for the good of the church. Maybe at some point it will be part of history.

the church several times in high-level meetings, where I had to respond to the actions of individual members or particular congregations.

In that context lies the opportunity to experience true dependence on God and witness His power in seemingly impossible situations.

Yet, amid these circumstances, we were planning to establish an organization that encompassed over six hundred congregations and ninety thousand members; launch a national television channel; construct a hundred churches; and improve the infrastructure of several schools and youth camps. Additionally, we aimed to conduct an annual community service program supported by national TV and radio stations, with more than ten thousand volunteers participating over one week. How was it possible to even consider all of this under such conditions? And beyond that, to care for each member, many of whom struggled daily to get by with minimal food.

We leaders understood that our plans could not depend solely on analyzing our strengths, opportunities, weaknesses, and threats (SWOT). If we had relied only on these factors for evaluation and strategic planning, we would never (and I emphasize, NEVER) have made these decisions in our year-end meeting.

We moved forward with these decisions because God, through His Holy Spirit, had convinced us of this purpose and assured us of victory. This conviction motivated and inspired an action that transcended human possibilities. It was not the first time God had placed a burden on us, nor would it be the last. Our challenge was to understand and apply the secret to seeing God's kingdom bless His people.

The church, a bastion of the kingdom of God

I agree that God has called His church to be the light of the world. But many times, the obstacles around us can limit the manifestation of divine glory in our ministry. Can this change? Absolutely! After witnessing all that the Almighty has done and continues to do, I understand that if we truly hope to see the power of God's kingdom in our churches, congregations must recover their biblical sense of purpose—the very reason they were founded.

Scripture clearly presents the different expressions and metaphors to try to explain what it means spiritually: the union of two or three believers who have been called by God in an ekklesía[36]or church. The apostle Paul refers to the church as "the body of Christ" (1 Corinthians 12:27-28); the "temple of the Lord" (Ephesians 2:21); the "glory of the Lord" (2 Corinthians 3:18, Ephesians 1:12, 3:21); the "family of God" (Ephesians 2:19); the "wisdom of God" (Ephesians 3:10) and the "fullness of God."

These images and meanings provide a deeper understanding of what God intended the church to be and how it should act in the world—not to mention Christ's words describing His followers as the salt of the earth and the light of the world (Matthew 5:13-16).

These expressions related to the church present a vision of God's presence and His kingdom within the community of believers. This divine authority and heavenly manifestation is powerfully conveyed in Christ's words: "I will *give you the keys of the kingdom* of heaven, and *whatever you bind on earth will be bound in heaven, and whatever you loose on earth will be loosed in heaven.*" (Matthew 16:19, emphasis added). When I read this text, I see not only the keys of knowledge and truth (Luke 11:52) or the power to prohibit or allow (Matthew 18:18), but also the delegated authority (Isaiah 22:22) to intercede in Christ (Ephesians 2:5-6) before God (Matthew 18:18, 20, 21:22, John 14:13, 1 Peter 2:9-10; Revelation 1:6-8, 5:10). I invite you to examine these texts with prayerful attention and care.

However, over the years, the church has adjusted its understanding and approach to its responsibility. Its power, presence, and influence have diminished. What was an overwhelming force in the New Testament—capable

---

[36]*Ekklesía*It is a Greek word that means "public assembly or gathering of people of a town in a religious, political or informal sense." John D. Barry and others, Faithlife Study Bible (Bellingham, WA: Lexham Press, 2016).

of disrupting kingdoms and empires—today seems out of step, reduced to ceremonies lacking power. Where is the fire? Where is the power? Where does the wisdom and fullness of God reside within the congregation?

What could be the cause? I once read an article that, drawing on David Moberg's five stages of religious organization, suggested that the church begins to lose its strength when it enters the fourth stage of institutionalization.[37]

These stages chart a path of growth, development, aging, and ultimately, death. Why? Over-institutionalization often leads to disintegration, marked by formalism, bureaucracy, and the pursuit of self-interest by various groups. Conflict with the world is replaced by tolerance and social conformity. Confidence in leadership is lost as needs go unmet—a topic that calls for deeper study and analysis.

The question, then, is: How can we prevent the church from losing its prophetic and divine purpose? How can we rekindle its power, legacy, and spirit?

Christ described the church at Sardis: "I know your works; you have a name for being alive, but you are dead" (Revelation 3:1, emphasis added), and the church at Laodicea: "You say, 'I am rich; I have become wealthy and have need of nothing,' and you do not know that you are wretched, miserable, poor, blind, and naked" (Revelation 3:17, emphasis added). Both texts reveal that God sees the congregation's appearance as different from its reality, form apart from substance. This is why the manifestation of God's kingdom is often absent in congregations.

The question we must ask, then, is: How can we return the church to its original power, when in its simplicity it made empires tremble? It is crucial to spend time reflecting on these thoughts—especially for the leaders whom God

---

[37] The five stages are: Incipient organization, Formal organization, Maximum efficiency, Institutionalization and Disintegration

has called and entrusted with His church today. How can the church become the center of God's kingdom on earth?

This question is not easy to answer; even addressing all its aspects would take time. But let me outline some areas that we as leaders must attend to in order to grow God's kingdom within our congregations.

Will they live?

"He said to me, 'Mortal, can these bones live?' I answered, 'O Lord God, you know." (Ezekiel 37:3). The reality within your congregation is not greater than what God can accomplish in it. Many leaders assume their congregations' condition is beyond recovery—they seem like dry bones. However, what you think will happen is not what determines the outcome; rather, it is what God knows!

This concept must be clear in the minds of church members and leaders who hope to see a resurrection or revival within their congregations. Life and death are in God's hands alone.

1. Avoid speaking about church problems as if they are unchangeable (Ezekiel 37:3).
2. Believe in God's power to transform any situation in any congregation (Matthew 19:26).
3. Remember, God will work according to your faith: "According to your faith let it be done to you." (Matthew 9:29).
4. Purify your heart of self-interest, which can deceive and weaken your faith, limiting your actions and hindering the full purpose of your leadership. Don't seek to protect your personal interests, reputation, or position—these motivations often misalign with the mission and make us hesitant, slow, or reluctant to confront problems and challenges (Jeremiah 17:9).

The victorious church

The only way to revive the church is to reestablish it on the original principles that allowed the Holy Spirit's manifestation. I want to spend more time on this aspect because it is the focus of this chapter. It wasn't only about what they did but what they believed. Their actions were firmly grounded in these beliefs. So, what are they?

They were in another sphere of struggle

The early church understood that their struggle took place in a supernatural sphere where they confronted Satan, the "the spirit who now works in the sons of disobedience" (Ephesians 2:2).

Paul stated in that same letter to the Ephesians: "For we do not wrestle against flesh and blood, but against principalities, against powers, against the rulers of the darkness of this age, *against spiritual hosts of wickedness in the heavenly places*" (Ephesians 6:12, emphasis added). When Paul speaks of "flesh and blood," he refers clearly to human beings (Matthew 16:17; Galatians 1:16). But when he mentions *"spiritual hosts of wickedness,"* he points to the powers of darkness (Colossians 1:13) representing the "ruler of this world" (John 12:31), the devil and his angels (1 John 5:19, Ephesians 4:27, 2 Corinthians 2:11, James 4:7).

Peter similarly stated: "Be sober, be vigilant; because your adversary the devil walks about like a roaring lion, seeking whom he may devour." (1 Peter 5:8). These verses reveal the early church's understanding of their true enemy and the battleground on which they fought.

Imagine what it meant for them to lack a meeting place, to be regarded as a sect, to live without financial resources, and to face persecution from both the Jews and the Roman government. Were there even realistic chances of survival? None. Yet, despite these obstacles, they moved forward victoriously. Why? Could it be related to what we are discussing here? What do you think? Today, e have resources, freedom from persecution in many countries, and meeting paces. Many of our members even hold positions in governments. But in some laces, churches still face the threat of decline if growth rates continue as they re.

Through the centuries, that same spirit has remained in the true church. hey didn't have large temples or resources, yet they survived by faith, even in he remotest areas. In contrast, today, with freedom from persecution and an bundance of resources, the truth seems, in some places, to be losing its elevance.

The Protestant conviction that Luther drew from Paul's letter to the Romans, that "the just shall live by faith" (Romans 1:17), has faded. Paul also peaks of "the good fight of faith" (1 Timothy 6:12), emphasizing that the early church's struggle was not based on human strategies or resources but on faith n God and His kingdom in Christ (Ephesians 1:20-22; Colossians 1:13, 2:10).

Reflect on this for a moment: Could today's church resources have become an obstacle, rather than a strength as intended? I am not suggesting that resources are inherently harmful—only that they must not distract us from our real source of power.

Could it be that the church has changed its battlefield? Have they shifted their trust from God to their own abilities? The prophet Jeremiah described this reality with a powerful metaphor: "For My people have committed two evils: They have forsaken Me, the fountain of living waters, And hewn themselves cisterns—*broken cisterns* that can hold no water." (Jeremiah 2:13, emphasis added).

The "cisterns" in this verse refer to underground tanks that Israelites would dig to collect rainwater, a necessity in Palestine's dry climate. Cisterns and wells were of utmost importance, and they would fill with rainwater channeled from rooftops. Their construction was critical; if poorly sealed, water would leak.

There is, of course, a stark contrast between the water stored in a cistern and flowing well.[38]

The early church had not yet made this shift. They knew their main battl was not between themselves or with the Roman Empire but against darl principalities trying to destroy the church's faith. They understood that thei only resource was God, His power, and His kingdom.

It is tragic that today, in many cases, the church has forgotten this reality striving to win converts or strengthen marriages and member commitment without first addressing the spiritual battle within each heart.

Knowledge in fields such as management, leadership, psychology sociology, physics, and neurology can help immensely. But they cannot resolve the root problem, a spiritual issue with its deepest solution in what Chris accomplished for us on the cross when He took the decree that opposed us and nailed it there (Colossians 2:14-17). This truth brings liberation and salvation; i is the essence of the gospel's good news. We must learn to evaluate things no by human measures but by the Spirit.

Jesus understood this reality when He said to Peter, "Get behind me, Satan" (Matthew 16:23). We see what happened here: Jesus Christ understood that He wasn't merely confronting Peter's idea, but Satan himself, who *covertly attempted* to dissuade Him from His mission. The apostle John also wrote that we must test the spirits to discern if they are from God (1 John 4:6).

I know that right now, you're reflecting deeply on this reality in your life. You wonder if this is why you can't seem to win this fight, and if this is also why your church does not receive the grace of God.

We need to believe. I understand the feeling of helplessness before challenges and trials with no solution in sight. But it was in those moments that

---

[38]https://www.mundobiblicoelestudiodesupalabra.com/2016/02/cisternas-rotas.html.

I realized all my studies, experience, and position were nothing but empty cisterns. Recognizing this turned my pain into hope. Nothing is more difficult than watching your world fall apart and not knowing how to fix it. That's when *you understand where the true source of living water is for your life.*

How will we fight this spiritual fight?

Jesus clearly presented the secret of his victory: "I will no longer talk much with you, for the ruler of this world is coming, and he has nothing in Me" (John 14:30). At first, I didn't fully understand this statement and saw it only as an exclusive experience of Jesus. But after reflecting deeply, I realized why Satan couldn't defeat Christ. The answer lies in the text: "he has nothing in me." This means that Satan had no foothold or way to deceive the Savior. So what does this mean for us? We can be defeated by Satan when we haven't confessed our sins. In other words, Satan's power is neutralized when we are freed from sin.

Dear reader, supernatural victory over spiritual forces begins with our freedom and forgiveness in Christ. (Take a moment to reflect on this concept, first introduced in chapter 2.) This is why Revelation describes the remnant as those who have conquered in this spiritual battle, saying: "And they overcame him because of the blood of the Lamb and the word of their testimony" (Revelation 12:11). This experience of victory is what Christ and the apostles described as "being in Christ," where we live under the authority and kingdom of God (Revelation 12:10).

Those who are in Christ can experience the promise of Christ: "If you abide in Me, and My words abide in you, you will ask what you desire, and it shall be done for you." (John 15:7). "And whatever you ask in My name, that I will do, that the Father may be glorified in the Son. [14] If you ask anything in My name, I will do it." (John 14:13-14). We can call this experience: being in the plane or sphere of the kingdom of Christ.

It's one thing for a stranger to ask me for something, and another entirely when my own child makes the request. Can you see the difference in being within the sphere of God's kingdom? For a long time, I wrestled with how to pray with confidence, especially knowing I'd be heard, until I finally understood this truth.

Let me offer another illustration. Have you ever experienced what it feels like to be a foreigner? Those who are in a country not their own cannot demand aid, services, or respect for their rights in the same way as a citizen. The same is true in God's kingdom. As foreigners to God's kingdom, we cannot receive His gifts and grace in full measure. However, when we become part of His kingdom and gain citizenship, we then have the right to claim every promise that comes with this new identity.

When I look back on my relationship with God, I often see myself as more of a foreigner than a citizen—pleading for mercy but not realizing that victory and the promises made to citizens of God's kingdom are a reality in Christ. Paul expressed it clearly: "for all the promises of God in Him are Yes, and in Him Amen, to the glory of God through us" (2 Corinthians 1:20).

I agree with living as a foreigner in this world, enduring hardships for Christ. But our condition as members of God's supernatural kingdom is different. On this "plane," we are to act and feel like children of the King of kings, co-heirs with Christ, and—most importantly—representatives of that kingdom! The Lord Jesus referenced this spiritual authority when He told Peter and the disciples that whatever they bind on earth would be bound in heaven. He emphasized this authority again, saying that whatever we ask in His name, He will accomplish so that the Father may be glorified.

This transformation of spiritual condition—confessing our sins and uniting with Christ to become citizens of the kingdom—is what Satan fears most. Why? Because once we're on the plane of God's kingdom, we can confront and overcome him, even in this sinful world, where Jesus reigns supreme.

Ellen White expressed it this way:

There is nothing that Satan fears so much as that the people of God shall clear the way by removing every hindrance, *so that the Lord can pour out His*

Spirit upon a languishing church.... Every temptation, every opposing influence, whether open or secret, may be successfully resisted, "not by might, nor by power, but by my Spirit, saith the Lord of hosts" (Zechariah 4:6).[39]

By living within the "realm" of God's kingdom, the Christian leader can draw on God's power to elevate the church, guiding it into a spiritual experience characterized by victories, breakthroughs, and miracles that human efforts, knowledge, and strategies alone cannot achieve.

This is why it's crucial for leaders to first reflect on their own lives, making the necessary adjustments to apply these kingdom principles personally before guiding others to experience them as citizens of God's kingdom.

Being a kingdom citizen involves embracing both the cross and the throne, as we discussed earlier. The cross is where we acknowledge our limitations and accept Jesus as Savior; the throne is where we recognize Him as our sovereign King, actively working on our behalf. Remember, however: whether at the cross or the throne, the work is not ours—it is Christ's.

I just knelt in prayer, praising God for this truth and asking that it bring light, life, freedom, power, and miracles into your life as well.

Satan's greatest desire is to prevent the church, its members, and especially its leaders from reaching this "spiritual condition" within God's kingdom. He knows that if they do, we will witness barren deserts bloom and faith spread across the earth like wildfire. Was this not the experience of the apostolic church? More than relying on structures or programs, they were driven by the vision of being citizens of God's kingdom, claiming spiritual promises and gifts with the authority to bind and loose.

---

[39]Ellen G. White, Selected Messages 1:124 (1887), emphasis added.

Let us pray to Christ as King and Lord

Consider for a moment what occurred with the early church. After Peter and John were released from prison under strict orders not to speak in Jesus' name (Acts 4:18), the church gathered to confront the situation. What did they do? Here, we see the essence of operating on a different plane of struggle. The actions they took then defined their success, both in the past and for the future of the church.

Notice that we don't see the early church strategizing to negotiate or find a compromise. Nor do we see them focusing on improving relations or directly confronting leaders. (While these actions have value, they should not be the priority.) No, they were operating on a different level—another sphere, another kingdom! Not in the flesh but in the realm of Christ's kingdom, the same kingdom in which, "by faith in his name," the paralytic was healed, establishing the power of that name (Acts 3:16). What name? Paul clarifies: "therefore God also has highly exalted Him and given Him the name which is above every name, that at the name of Jesus every knee should bow, of those in heaven, and of those on earth, and of those under the earth, and that every tongue should confess that Jesus Christ is Lord, to the glory of God the Father" (Philippians 2:9-11).

So, what did the church do? They did one thing: they cried out to God praying, "Sovereign Lord" (Acts 4:24, New Revised Standard Version). Do you see it? At the very beginning of their prayer lies the faith and conviction they held—the spiritual condition through which God revealed His presence and power among them.

To them, God's sovereignty and Christ's authority were absolute realities and they surrendered entirely to this truth. When they sensed that the Kingdom of God was under threat, they pleaded fervently for God to empower them and stretch out His "hand" to reveal His power (Acts 4:29). They asked for an ever reater outpouring of God's Kingdom among them.[40] They pleaded for the pirit's power to boldly confront the threats from religious leaders forbidding hem to preach in the name of Christ.

What was unfolding here? On one level, they were confident that God vould hear and respond; on another, they understood themselves as participants a Christ's authority, empowered to request divine intervention. This was not a nere plea but a bold petition that laid claim to Christ's promise over their lives. They prayed, *"Consider their threats and enable your servants."* Do you see it? They vere effectively saying, "They aim to stop us, but here we stand, Your servants, eady to press on and fulfill our mission."

Now, I ask: is there a difference between this prayer and the ones we ypically offer in our churches? How do we pray? I'm convinced that if we ransform our approach to prayer—embracing a prayer experience that seeks to lign with the spiritual realm—the church will reach this higher "plane" and be :mpowered to advance "fair as the moon, clear as the sun, awesome as *an army* with banners" (Song of Solomon 6:10).

The battle of faith, the battle in the Spirit

Now, the most important question is this: Doesn't today's church need to confront the enemy's threats to our homes, lives, and ministries, pleading for God's empowerment to hold every inch of territory against him? I believe much of what we do in the church is helpful, but it's urgent for leaders to guide the church into experiencing prayer on the "plane" of the kingdom to achieve the victories of God's kingdom. Can you imagine what would happen in your congregation or area if you could pray as the apostolic church did?

---

[40]The prayer that Christ taught his disciples says: "Your kingdom come. "Your will be done on earth as it is in heaven" (Matthew 6:10). Shouldn't this also be our prayer?

No more frustrated leaders and lifeless churches

When Paul wrote to Philemon, he asked, "But, meanwhile, also prepare guest room for me, for I trust that *through your prayers I shall be granted to yo* (Philemon 1:22, emphasis added). In saying, *"through your prayers I shall be gran to you,"* Paul highlighted how, when God's children pray in the spiritual realr they can influence what happens in the natural world. This understanding shared by the early church leaders and congregation alike—was the true secr of their victory against Satan and his schemes.

So, this is essential: Do you think it's possible to see the kingdom's extern manifestation if it isn't first established in the heart? Impossible! Jes emphasized this when he declared, *"According to your faith* let it be to you (Matthew 9:29, emphasis added). We discussed this earlier in the chapter, b let's dig deeper.

What did Christ mean by this? That the kingdom of God is manifeste outwardly only when it has first taken root in the heart through faith. It essential for the believer to live the kingdom of God within. This experienc transcends outward actions; it centers on what we believe about Christ, our ro as His servants, and His sovereignty as Lord of Lords.

This spiritual depth moves both members and the church to pray nc merely for things, but for deliverance, for greater strength, and for the victor of God's kingdom over the enemy. Can you see how deep and powerful ou prayer can become?

Many only pray for what happens within the physical sphere of life, yet *th overlook that true victory is achieved in the spiritual sphere.* This is precisely what Pau meant when he emphasized, "for we do not wrestle against flesh and blood, bu against principalities, against powers, against the rulers of the darkness of thi age, against spiritual hosts of wickedness in the heavenly places" (Ephesian 6:12). Paul understood that what occurs in the physical realm is subject to wha transpires in the spiritual "realm." If we miss this, the church—our communit of believers—will lack the victories God intends, as it will rely more on physica actions than on spiritual power, on works rather than on faith.

Imagine two congregations. The first, which we'll call "trained and independent," knows all the right things to do. They are well-prepared, able to recite their strategies by heart, and diligently execute their plans. The second congregation, "capable and *dependent*," also has knowledge and experience but *relies on prayer and faith in divine power* as their greatest strength. They too design effective strategies, but they look to God for victory. Which of these two congregations will witness God's power? Often, we focus on human knowledge or resources, but the true difference in advancing God's kingdom lies in dependence on His power.

In apostolic times, many churches had highly trained individuals. However, Scripture tells us that in Antioch, Christians were ministering to the Lord and fasting when God revealed His will to appoint Paul and Barnabas (Acts 13:2). Would this have happened without *their attitude of reliance* and seeking God? This is the very reason why the ministries of Christ, Paul, and the apostles were marked by supernatural outcomes. Let us always remember: "Those who achieve the greatest results are *those who rely most implicitly upon the Almighty Arm.*"[41]

What needs to be done with the church?

What can we do as leaders to bring the church to that level or plane of experience, in which the power of the kingdom of God is realized in the hearts of the members and in the entire congregation? What do you need to do for your church to experience Pentecost? What can you do in the church? I share with you four personal and congregational actions, which I call: Get ready for the fight!

- It must be recognized that our true enemy is Satan (1 Peter 5:8).

---

[41] Ellen G. White, History of the Patriarchs and Prophets (Doral, FL: APIA, 2008), 509, emphasis added.

- Be freed from its satanic influence by confessing our sins and th
  be in Christ (Ephesians 2:5-6).
- Test the spirits through the Word of God so as not to be seduc
  and deceived by the enemy (1 John 4:1).
- Pray aware of the authority of Christ (Ephesians 1:18-22).

These actions, when assimilated into Christian life, will transform th
leader, the member, the entire church, and will take them to another level i
their spiritual experience. You will be prepared to enjoy the spiritual plane
condition that Ellen White says Satan fears most, because by exercising the
actions all paths of ignorance, sin, confusion and unbelief are cleared. What th
apostle Paul stated to the Corinthians will be fulfilled in our life and church::

> For though we walk in the flesh, we do not war according to the
> flesh. For the weapons of our warfare *are* not carnal but mighty in
> God for pulling down strongholds, casting down arguments and
> every high thing that exalts itself against the knowledge of God,
> bringing every thought into captivity to the obedience of Christ (2
> Corinthians 10:3 -5, emphasis added).

The insights above deepen our understanding of the power that unfolds i
prayer when one bows before the cross and sits on the throne—a
understanding introduced in the second chapter. Ignoring these profounc
practical truths will hinder us from experiencing God's power in our lives. Thi
absence becomes dire and urgent when the church as a whole fails to understan
or prepare for the spiritual battle required to overcome Satan and prepare fo
eternity. Understanding how to secure victories, achievable only through God'
supernatural intervention, is essential for us today.

Therefore, to experience the fullness of God's power in your life and in th
church, it is crucial to guide your life—and that of the church members—towar
embodying the same vision as the early church. Only this will lead to a spiritua
journey filled with victories beyond measure. Now, the four principles we have
explored must be lived out in the congregation in three specific ways.

Each congregation is a bastion from which the kingdom of God expands, and every Christian is a representative of that kingdom. The white horse, symbolizing the church's triumphant early period, represents its victory over forces intent on halting and destroying it (Revelation 6:2).

Three practices marked the life of the early church, which I refer to as the "Triple Custom: Fight the Battle of Faith." When the church embodies these actions, only one outcome is possible: the manifestation of God's power within the congregation.

1.   The temple or meeting place must fulfill its central purpose.

2.   The Christian must be equipped for the battle.

3.   They activated the kingdom's manifestation.

These three practices are vital to recreating the experiences of the disciples in the upper room and those of believers in the Great Awakening of the 19th century, which gave rise to the Seventh-day Adventist Church. What do these mean?

The temple or meeting place must fulfill its main function

This statement of Christ, recorded in all three gospels and directly referencing Isaiah, underscores the purpose of the temple as a place of prayer (Matthew 21:12-16; Luke 19:45-47; John 2:13-16; Isaiah 56:7). In the temple, meant for communion with God, Jesus encountered buyers, sellers, and money changers. Here, He made clear the primary purpose of this sacred space for His followers:

- "And He said to them, It is written, 'My house shall be called a house of prayer" (Matthew 21:13).
- "It is written, 'My house is a house of prayer," (Luke 19:46).

When we turn to the book of Acts, we see believers *gathered with a central focus on prayer*. Prayer wasn't a mere part of their agenda; it was the core experience that empowered them to engage their true enemy. Imagine if prayer in our churches today went beyond routine formalities. What if it became a powerful, communal effort led by pastors and church leaders who viewed it as central to their calling, just as the apostle Peter said: "but *we will give ourselves continually to prayer* and to the ministry of the word" (Acts 6:4, emphasis added)

It's time for both individuals and the church to engage in earnest spiritual battles, targeting areas where victories are needed. The early Christians prayed together, presenting their needs to God with faith that His kingdom would manifest through them. This faith empowered them to witness hearts transformed, lives healed, and their numbers multiplied, despite obstacles.

Now, imagine if prayer were also accompanied by fasting. Jesus taught His disciples that certain strongholds can only be overcome through the combined power of prayer and fasting (Matthew 17:21).

The Christian was equipped for the fight

The apostle Paul reflected on the nature of struggle in the book of Ephesians. He clearly described the clothing necessary for battle:

> Therefore take up the whole armor of God, that you may be able to withstand in the evil day, and having done all, to stand. Stand therefore, having girded your waist *with truth*, having put on the *breastplate of righteousness*, and having shod your feet with the preparation of the *gospel of peace*; above all, taking the *shield of faith* with which you will be able to quench all the fiery darts of the wicked one. And take the *helmet of salvation*, and the sword of the Spirit, which is the *word of God*; praying always with all prayer and supplication in the Spirit, being watchful to this end with all perseverance and supplication for all the saints. (Ephesians 6:13-18, emphasis added).

Dear reader, these verses should be the focus of your prayerful meditation and reflection. While a more extensive discussion would be needed to fully xplore their depth, the essential takeaway is this: God has equipped us with verything necessary to confront the enemy's attacks on our lives, His church, nd His kingdom. The Christian's struggle is not rooted in flesh and blood. This ruth must stay at the forefront! Only by recognizing this can we tear down trongholds (2 Corinthians 10:4). Without this understanding, we, along with he members and their families, risk remaining captives in a desert devoid of God's power.

Many enter the kingdom of God through baptism, yet continue to struggle carnally to overcome personal, social, church, and spiritual challenges. They come to know and apply countless strategies, but these efforts lack the divine power needed to "destroy" the strongholds they face. This is akin to when the fulfillment of prophecy was delayed in Daniel's time as he prayed for Jeremiah's words to come to pass (Daniel 10:2-14).

If we believe in the Word of God and the testimony of the conversation of Christ and the seventy[42] disciples, we will find it stated: "Lord, even the demons are subject to us in Your name. And He said to them, "I saw Satan fall like lightning from heaven. Behold, I give you the authority to trample on serpents and scorpions, and over all the power of the enemy, and nothing shall by any means hurt you." (Luke 10:17-20). What appears in this dialogue? t was not merely a battle; it was the triumph of servants sent by God to accomplish His work.

Years and centuries have passed, yet I am convinced that the power once given to the disciples remains available to His church today—if we have the faith to *abandon our reliance on the flesh* and step fully into the kingdom of faith.

As I write these words I know how much fear, doubt or skepticism can chain your heart. But think, isn't that what has stopped us? And furthermore,

---

[42]It is important to highlight that the power of God to accomplish the task was not limited to the apostles, but all the disciples could experience the reality of the kingdom of God in their life and ministry.

what about the new generation that not only doubts, but trivializes these tex as a mythological story? The question is when Christ returns, "will he find fai on earth?" (Luke 18:8).

My dear reader, in addition to prayer, the Word of God served as th foundation for both Daniel, who held fast to Jeremiah's promise, and Paul, wh wielded the sword of the Spirit to triumph in their battles against Satan. Th Word of God must be more than text to study, memorize, or defend; it mu become an anticipated promise, a trusted prophecy, a decree of the kingdom c God and the Lord Jesus Christ. This Word should be our foundation, keepir our thoughts anchored on the invisible and enabling us to prevail by faith. No is the time to claim God's promises with fervor and faith—in the church, withi the family, and in our personal lives—through dedicated prayer! For this reasor Ellen White insisted: "When the Word of God is sent home to the human hea: by the Holy Spirit, it is mighty to the pulling down of the strongholds of Satan."

Let's activate the manifestation of the kingdom

The third and final experience of the early church that allowed it to receiv power to overcome and witness the presence of the kingdom of God was th unity among its members. This unity enabled them to advance wit. unprecedented strength. In Acts 2, we read that when the Spirit descended, the were of one accord and together. Two chapters later, upon hearing the apostles report, they lifted their voices "with one accord" to God (Acts 4:24). Such unit empowered the church to secure great victories and receive answers to thei prayers.

Christ promised, "Again I say to you that if two of you agree on earth concerning anything that they ask, it will be done for them by My Father ir

---

[43] Ellen G. White, Being Like Jesus, 348.

eaven" (Matthew 18:19). This divine promise holds as much power today as it id when Jesus spoke it to His disciples.

A boundless spiritual experience awaits you if you seek unity through the pirit of God, resolve your differences, forgive those who have wronged you, nd confess your faults to your neighbor. A church that embraces this spiritual eality will undoubtedly experience the presence of God, as well as answers to heir prayers from the heavenly Father. Do any of these conditions need to be net among us to witness the victories we yearn for in our lives and ongregations?

The answer, I'm sure, lies within your heart. We can continue to battle with ur "armies" and our "strength," but you know the result—continuing in this lesert without seeing the power of God. It's time for that to change in your life nd in the church. It's time to witness God's limitless power. Remember what ²eter assured us: "as His divine power has given to us *all things* that pertain *to life and godliness*" (2 Peter 1, emphasis added). Amen.

Assessment

To close this chapter, I present an evaluation to assess the application of these principles in your ministry and congregation.

Evaluation of the Church and Leaders in Implementing the Victory Plan for the Battle of Faith

1. Does each member of the church recognize that their struggle is spiritual and that repentance and confession of sins are necessary to pray with an awareness of Christ's authority? Yes____ No____
2. Is prayer, along with the Word of God, the central focus in every worship gathering? Yes____ No____

3. Is each member committed to strengthening their faith throug personal prayer and participating in corporate prayer gatherings in t congregation? Yes____ No____

4. Are you actively praying and working to foster harmony and uni among all members by encouraging confession and mutu forgiveness? Yes____ No____

5

The leader's approach: THE SECRET OF MULTIPLICATION

The director's words surprised me, "Is that what you say happens in our congregation? That's just how we are here!" He had a kind face, a broad forehead, and an easy smile, always willing to lend a hand. He was genuinely one of the few rare exceptions in the place—a good Christian—but...

Let me remind you, I was in a district where, for nearly two decades, the congregations hadn't grown. The pioneer leaders did what they knew: repeating the same plans over and over, hoping for different results. However, besides the lack of growth, a lack of unity among congregations and leaders posed a major challenge.

Except for the first elder and a few others, most were preoccupied with debates over various matters. They argued about doctrines; the styles and methods of conducting programs and ceremonies; who got to participate on the platform; decisions made by the church board; who was the pastor's favorite; what the young pastor's wife was doing; why the pastor didn't inform them about certain actions or decisions. And they would relay everything (and I mean *everything*, even without the help of smartphones and social media) to one another with remarkable speed. There were many more issues—let your imagination fill in the gaps!

Just a few days after I arrived, a member with a gravelly voice and a stern expression told me that if I wanted to accomplish anything, I should have to be "*in the very center of it all*". I haven't forgotten his advice.

The group director's words, "Is that what you say happens in our congregation? That's just how we are here," accompanied by his tolerant smile, reflected a resigned acceptance of their reality up to that point. And, indeed, this man had the patience of Job! Practically, he and another brother were the only ones who could exercise leadership. The rest were engaged in a "holy" war to assert their opinions, claim positions, control "their" church, or outdo each other in perceived righteousness.

If I wanted to see change in that congregation, can you imagine what needed to happen? Yes, I think you can imagine it. But first, let me share about Paul and the secret of his ministry, and then I'll return to what happened in these congregations.

The success of the apostle Paul

When we closely examine the successful ministry of the apostle Paul, we find that one of his greatest secrets was his choice to follow the model of Christ Jesus. Formerly known as Saul, he could have easily followed the traditions of Gamaliel and the esteemed teachers at whose feet he learned. But instead, he chose to walk in the footsteps of Jesus, building his ministry on the example Christ set. Notice I emphasize the model of Christ, for many have lost their ministry by following other paths. Paul's wise decision led to a ministry unparalleled in productivity, reach, and legacy, surpassing the works of his contemporaries and even those who succeeded him.

I remember vividly that before I grasped this truth, I was entirely absorbed in being a "*do-it-all*" leader in my congregation. When I refer to a "*do-it-all*" leader I mean someone who spends most of their time racing from one event to the next, focused on covering every detail. For a long time, I was dedicated, with passion and sacrifice, to discovering the "right way" to minister effectively. But I hadn't yet understood the foundational principle that would transform my ministry.

In the early years, when I was young and full of energy, I could handle many commitments. But as the years went by and my strength waned, I realized that if I wanted to remain both efficient and, more importantly, effective, I needed to adjust my approach. This realization came when I encountered Paul's words to the brothers and leaders of the church in Ephesus, words that reshaped my ministry perspective.

Paul wrote: "And He Himself gave some to be apostles, some prophets, some evangelists, and some pastors and teachers, for the equipping of the saints for the work of ministry, for the edifying of the body of Christ, till we all come to the unity of the faith and of the knowledge of the Son of God, to a perfect man, to the measure of the stature of the fullness of Christ;" (Ephesians 4:11-13).

In carefully examining this passage, we see a description of the various leaders in biblical times. Paul is referring to church leaders—apostles, prophets, evangelists, pastors, and teachers—who played crucial roles in the apostolic church. Paul's words are striking because he clearly defines the primary task of these leaders: *equipping the saints for the work of ministry!*

This emphasis from Paul stands in stark contrast to how leadership is often categorized today. Modern books and studies on leadership tend to define it as a role focused solely on motivation, organization, and inspiration, supported by positional authority, charisma, or experience. However, we see here that early church leaders were focused on a different kind of leadership—one centered on preparing, training, and equipping members to carry out a ministry for Christ.

Paul's model was not about discarding those who weren't prepared but about investing in them, training and equipping them for ministry. This approach was precisely how Christ led His apostles, perfecting them for their roles in ministry.

Perfecting for the work of the ministry

It is important that we understand that the word ministry is referring to service. The term ministry comes from the Greek *diakonia* and can be translated as service.[44]

Some texts that talk about *service* in the New Testament	
Acts 1:17	For he was numbered with us and obtained a part in this ministry.
Acts 1:25	To take part in this ministry and apostleship from which Judas by transgression fell, that he might go to his own place.
1 Corinthians 12:5	There are differences of ministries, but the same Lord.
Colossians 4:17	And say to Archippus, "Take heed to the ministry which you have received in the Lord, that you may fulfill it."
2 Timothy 4:5	But you be watchful in all things, endure afflictions, do the work of an evangelist, fulfill your ministry.
2 Timothy 4:11	Only Luke is with me. Get Mark and bring him with you, for he is useful to me for ministry.

It is deeply striking that, when God led the people of Israel out of Egypt through It is deeply striking that when God led the people of Israel out of Egypt through Moses, He instructed Pharaoh to let His people go so they could serve Him (Exodus 7:16, 9:13). What does this mean? In both the Old and New Testaments, heaven's purpose in calling its children is to empower them for ministry.

---

[44]The term means service, help, role or position of service, arrangement for the support of another, contribution of money to help someone in need, serving food and drinks. See James Swanson, *Dictionary of Biblical Languages with Semantic Domains: Greek (New Testament)*(Oak Harbor, MI: Logos Research Systems, 1997).

By carefully analyzing this text, we observe that the purpose is to perfect the saints so they can fulfill their ministry. In other words, the fundamental purpose of leadership is to develop the gifts and talents within church members, using the Holy Spirit's work in their hearts to move them from one experience to another, one area of knowledge to another, and one skill to another, all for building up the body of Christ.

From this text, we understand a cause-and-effect relationship in the ministry of church leaders. The cause is the leaders' work in perfecting the saints; the result or effect is the building up of the body of Christ.

In other words, to build up the body of Christ, leaders must fulfill the ministry of perfecting the saints (the called ones) for service. Thus, the body of Christ, or the church, will be perfected when leaders fulfill this ministry.

This type of leadership can be called the spiritual empowerment of the church member. Reflecting on this text and understanding what the apostle Paul was communicating to church leaders and members opened a new horizon before me. From that moment, I realized that my work as a leader had to be centered on equipping each church member, empowering the believer in Christ to carry out ministry for God.

Some church leaders may view members simply as followers, spectators, or believers. However, when we consider the biblical paradigm of leadership, it becomes clear that *leading members goes far beyond creating followers*. God's expectation for building up His body on earth is that each of His members will become effective, efficient servants in ministry for Him.

Do you see why leaders who desire to see radical change in their ministry must apply the apostle Paul's leadership model? Doing this and nothing else will place your ministry and leadership on a path that will lead to the same results achieved through this principle in the life and ministry of the apostle Paul.

If you sincerely want this to happen, you will need to focus your ministry, investing whatever is necessary, on one central task in the spiritual and biblical leadership you exercise in your congregation: equipping of the saints for the work of ministry.

To achieve this goal, it will be necessary to commit time to training and empowering church members. Additionally, you will need to invest resources for this purpose. Above all, keep in mind the expected outcome in each member's growth. As a leader, envision the goal God has for each member. Perfection in the service of God is His divine purpose for every church member and believer!

The Perfection of the Believer

The Holy Spirit's work in perfecting His children to the stature of Christ involves addressing several areas, from cultivating the fruit of the Spirit to utilizing gifts for His service. In the context of this book—focusing on the revival, growth, and prosperity of the church—we'll explore how those perfected as God's instruments can lead others to Christ. Jesus described His disciples as "fishers of men," emphasizing their purpose in drawing others to Him.

I am also convinced that this path requires developing the fruits of the Spirit alongside exercising one's God-given talents.

We can outline the growth or development of members in service to God, as disciples of Christ, in three stages. The first stage of a church member's spiritual growth can be called the *Believer* stage. For a more in-depth exploration, see *Leadership that Transforms: Secrets of Christian Discipleship*.

1.   Believer stage.

We could define the nominal believer as someone who accepts the gospel of Jesus Christ and adheres to its doctrines, yet does not actively participate in sharing the gospel or serving with their gifts. Such believers may recognize God's work in their lives and understand His blessings, but they do not actively share these experiences and blessings with those around them. An example of this type of member would be the multitudes that followed Christ during His ministry on earth. These followers witnessed and benefited from Christ's miracles; however, they did not engage closely, as did the apostles or the seventy who actively shared the gospel.

This type of nominal believer does not experience the reality of what Jesus said:

> And these signs will follow those who believe: In My name they will cast out demons; they will speak with new tongues; they will take up serpents; and if they drink anything deadly, it will by no means hurt them; they will lay hands on the sick, and they will recover. So then, after the Lord had spoken to them, He was received up into heaven, and sat down at the right hand of God. And they went out and preached everywhere, the Lord working with them and confirming the word through the accompanying signs. Amen. (Mark 16:17-20).

To reach this stage, a person transitions from unbelief to belief. However, their faith remains at the level of intellectual acceptance and partial surrender. They are neither far from God nor close enough to be actively used in His service. These believers are those who have accepted Christ solely as their personal Savior.

2. Disciple stage.

A disciple is someone who, beyond believing in Christ as their Savior, accepts Him as Lord and is committed to sharing their faith and using their gifts according to God's purpose for their life. This individual has developed an intimate relationship with God, yielding to His will, and allowing the Holy Spirit to lead and use them in ways that inspire others to believe in and follow the gospel of Christ. Disciples actively listen to, understand, and obey God's voice.

An example of this group of members could be Ananias and the early disciples of Christ:

> If anyone comes to Me and does not hate his father and mother, wife and children, brothers and sisters, yes, and his own life also, he cannot be My disciple. And whoever does not bear his cross and come after Me cannot be My disciple. For which of you, intending to build a tower, does not sit down first and count the cost, whether he has enough to finish it— lest, after he has laid the foundation, and is not able to finish, all who see it begin to mock him, saying, 'This man began to build and was not able to finish'? Or what king, going to make war against another king, does not sit down first and consider whether he is able with ten thousand to meet him who comes against him with twenty thousand? Or else, while the other is still a great way off, he sends a delegation and asks conditions of peace. So likewise, whoever of you does not forsake all that he has cannot be My disciple. (Luke 14: 26-33).

Another example of disciples can be found in the two demon-possessed men from Gadara, the Samaritan woman, and Philip—each transformed by their encounter with Christ and willing to become what God called them to be. In contrast, individuals like the rich young ruler and Ananias and Sapphira illustrate those who remained only believers, unable to transition fully into discipleship. These latter individuals believed, but they were not ready to commit themselves entirely to following Christ.

3. Leading disciple or discipling leader stage.

This type of person makes disciples and is responsible for them. As we can see, the discipling leader has not only moved beyond being a believer; they are also fully willing to serve God in winning others. But beyond that, such a person serves as a guide for the conversion and transformation of others into believers and disciples of Christ Jesus.

This type of discipling or transformative leadership exemplified the style of our Lord Jesus Christ and the apostle Paul. They were leaders, mentors to other disciples, those who perfected the saints for ministry. A detailed study of Christ's method was presented in the book *Leadership that Transforms*.

Jesus declared, as recorded in Matthew 10:24-25: "A disciple is not above his teacher, nor a servant above his master. It is enough for a disciple that he be like his teacher, and a servant like his master..."

This statement clearly shows that Christ's leadership focused on guiding disciples to a perfected level of service, aiming to elevate them to the same level as the work He performed. Christ's words make it unmistakably clear that the purpose of leadership—be it the prophet, teacher, pastor, or evangelist—is to guide disciples to mirror themselves in character and purpose... striving to be like Christ!

When leaders grasp this truth, their ministry is transformed. The moment one begins to experience the impact of applying this principle in their ministry, the results are profound. Could there be any other result? Imagine what would happen if your church dedicated itself to perfecting saints for ministry. I am confident the results would far surpass anything previously experienced.

Let me illustrate what it means to apply this principle and the outcomes it brings.

Suppose we attend a university to train as Physical Education teachers. During our studies, we amass substantial knowledge. Upon graduation, we hold a certificate confirming our expertise in anatomy, effective exercise routines, metabolic function, proper nutrition, and the regulations governing sports and exercise.

All that knowledge now resides in our minds, ready to be shared with those we teach or train. However, simply having this knowledge doesn't guarantee that we, as Physical Education teachers, will benefit. What do I mean? Reflecting on my student years, I remember some Physical Education teachers who knew everything about their bodies and sports, yet their own bodies and skills didn reflect the application of this knowledge. Does that sound familiar?

Now, if we go to a gym, we may lack deep understanding of anatomy routines, metabolic functions, and nutrition. However, we don't go there to si and accumulate knowledge; we go to exercise. As a result, our bodies improv in response to the effort and routines we perform. This means we experienc the benefits of exercise, even if we don't know the names of the techniques.

If leaders and members view church gatherings like attending a universit solely to gain knowledge, the outcome will be limited. The true significance o attending church is not merely to gather knowledge but to seek the power to serve God. This was precisely why the Pharisees, in Jesus' time, failed to truly experience the kingdom of God. Their aim was merely to fill their minds with the letter of the law, without exercising or living by the spirit of that letter.

The church is the living body of Christ

As we have seen, the church should function more like a gymnasium than a university. Paul explains that Christ is the head, and each member has a unique and vital role in His body, the church (1 Corinthians 12:12-27).

In the early church, those who led were often simple fishermen—men who hadn't attended college or earned degrees but knew firsthand what it meant to live in the kingdom of God. They hadn't received complex instruction filled with technical language or endless references to famous scholars. Instead, they had touched, seen, and experienced the truths they shared with others. They had been in a "spiritual gym," developing God's Spirit within their lives and gaining practical knowledge of what it meant to experience the power of the kingdom.

Have you felt frustrated because you lack more of God's power in your life? Have you wondered why you can't experience what the apostles did? Have you felt discouraged because, despite your knowledge, you experience little power?

These questions share a common answer: the church needs to transform into a place where each member can grow and be perfected in the image and likeness of Christ Jesus, not merely a place to accumulate knowledge.

By embracing this principle and applying this truth, we can see the same results that Christ, the apostles, and the early church saw. Personally, understanding and implementing this principle allows us to experience transformation and growth in serving God, both in our lives and within our church communities. Why? The answer is clear: discipleship, as Christ intended, isn't just about knowing or accepting a doctrine—it's about living out a mission.[45]

Three questions that *empower* the member

Let me explain the three questions that, when answered, lead to empowering a member and developing them into a disciple of Christ:

1. What will we do?
2. How will we do it?
3. With what authority and power will we do it?

I emphasize, these three questions guide each member's growth in ministry within God's kingdom and in experiencing God's power in their life.

The goal of leaders who are guided by biblical principles is that, through their service, members' lives are transformed. Could it be that today's church leaders need to realize that church is not merely something we declare but something we embody? If not, the more time pastors and elders spend on the pulpit, the more time members will spend sitting in the pews. Embracing this

---

[45]Rodríguez, A leadership that transforms, 118.

perspective will undoubtedly bring the kingdom of God to life in each member and their congregation.

Can we imagine what would happen if we applied this principle in our congregations? The growth of God's kingdom comes solely from the spiritual growth of each church member. Therefore, every member should be invited to commit to a life of continual growth in spiritual discipleship.

Member Commitment

As we have already noted, the leader's vision and dedication demand a reciprocal commitment from the member. Leadership development thrives as a system supported by two essential pillars: the commitment of the leader and the commitment of the member. These two pillars form the foundation for advancing the manifestation of God's kingdom within the congregation.

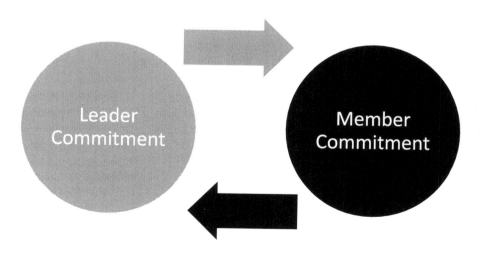

Do you remember when Jesus called the disciples to follow Him and be His apprentices? That simple act reflected the leader's desire and commitment.

What did it mean? When a leader actively seeks and calls disciples, he demonstrates a genuine commitment to biblical leadership. In response, by accepting the challenge to follow the teacher, the disciple reveals a commitment to learning and doing whatever the teacher asks.

When a person is baptized, they may mistakenly think they've achieved the goal set by God's call. They might believe they should merely accumulate knowledge while sitting in the church pew, listening to teachings and observing programs. However, each church member needs to understand that baptism is not the endpoint of their faith journey. On the contrary, it is the first small step on a longer path toward spiritual maturity. This is why those invited to be baptized must understand that, post-baptism, they begin a spiritual journey with the purpose of becoming like Jesus, living like Jesus, and acting like Jesus.

For this reason, every church member needs to be invited—both generally and individually—to commit to ongoing spiritual growth. As leaders, we may assume this is understood and neglect to emphasize it as a central part of our ministry. However, if we hope to see God's growth in our congregation, we must make this call to discipleship a vital aspect of our leadership.

In observing Christ's ministry, we see that the call to commit to discipleship is a prominent theme in the gospels. Each gospel, in one way or another, records Christ's invitation to discipleship. Careful observation shows that those called to be Christ's disciples and later apostles had already experienced baptism. And while baptism marks the beginning of discipleship, every church member must be invited again to commit—not merely as a believer but as a true disciple of Jesus Christ.

What does commitment to discipleship mean?

When a new member commits to discipleship, they are deciding to:

1. Attend training or discipleship development meetings.
2. Partner with a spiritual development mentor, such as a missionary couple.
3. Conduct a monthly self-assessment of spiritual growth and discipleship in their life.
4. Be evaluated by a mentor, small group leader, or elder regarding their spiritual development.

As shown, the church member commits to advancing in their spiritual life. To achieve this, they will participate in specific activities, like the "training gym," to grow in spirit and gain strength. They will also have a fellow disciple as a companion and receive guidance from spiritual leaders. However, the most essential aspect is the self-assessment that the disciple conducts to reflect on their spiritual progress and growth.

The purpose of this member growth will focus on ten areas, each requiring a commitment to achieve a holistic development grounded in the kingdom of God's fundamental principles. The ultimate aim for each member is to be like Jesus.

Ellen White stated: "Christ is waiting with longing desire for the manifestation of Himself in His church. When the character of Christ shall be perfectly reproduced in His people, then He will come to claim them as His own."[46]

And he also placed great emphasis on this solemn purpose that every church member should have:

Do you, my brethren and sisters, inquire: What model shall we copy? I do not point you to great and good men, but to the world's Redeemer. If we would have the true missionary spirit we must be imbued with the love of Christ; we must look to the Author and Finisher of our faith, study His

---

[46]Ellen G. White, Last Day Events (Boise, ID: Pacific Press, 1992), 39.

character, cultivate His spirit of meekness and humility, and walk in His footsteps.[47]

The metaphor of Christ

Under these two pillars—the commitment of the leader and the commitment of the member—the Holy Spirit will accomplish His purpose in building the body of Christ. Jesus spoke about growth in the spiritual life, saying, "For the earth yields crops by itself: first the blade, then the head, after that the full grain in the head" (Mark 4:28)"

The purpose is to achieve the integral growth of each church member. The greatest joy of a leader is witnessing the Holy Spirit working within each heart, like yeast, causing the kingdom of God to grow within the disciple.

To reach this goal, the discipling leader must commit to the following actions:

1. *Pray and Fast*

Let me share the following Scriptures, which clearly show how this principle was powerfully applied in the life of Paul and the apostles, producing incredible results:

"But we will give ourselves continually to prayer and to the ministry of the word" (Acts 6:4).

As a discipling leader, structure each day's itinerary by considering these questions: How much time will I dedicate to intercessory prayer? Do I know the

---

[47]Ellen G. White, Testimonies , tomo 5, 385.

specific needs of church members to bring before the Lord? I invite you to reflect on these texts and see how prayer permeated Paul's life:

"For God is my witness, whom I serve with my spirit in the gospel of His Son, that without ceasing I make mention of you always in my prayers" (Romans 1:9).

"I thank God, whom I serve with a pure conscience as my forefathers did, as without ceasing I remember you in my prayers night and day" (2 Timothy 1:3).

Reading and absorbing these words, we can feel the fervor and passion with which the apostle poured his heart out to God for the growth of His kingdom in the hearts of the believers. We often focus on Paul's powerful preaching ministry and forget that much of his time was spent in imprisonment, where he could only send letters and pray. His letters testify that he devoted most of his time to prayer.

If we ask why his ministry was so successful and powerful, the answer lies in plain sight. Today's leaders need to embody this principle! The church needs leaders who practice it.

2. Visit Members Monthly

After prayer, member visitation is one of the most effective ways to foster transformation and inspire members in their spiritual growth. I am deeply moved by how Paul described this part of his ministry to the elders in Ephesus, reflecting on his service with a profound sense of urgency:

"Therefore be alert, remembering that for three years I did not cease night or day to admonish everyone with tears" (Acts 20:31).

This powerful statement reflects Paul's dedication to personally visiting and encouraging members, day or night, with a heart full of compassion. I picture Paul going from home to home, sharing encouragement, guidance, and heartfelt admonition. Ellen White wrote:

As the shepherd of the flock he [the minister] should care for the sheep and the lambs, searching out the lost and straying, and bringing them back to the fold. He should visit every family, not merely as a guest to enjoy their hospitality, but to inquire into the spiritual condition of every member of the household. His own soul must be imbued with the love of God; then by kindly courtesy he may win his way to the hearts of all, and labor successfully for parents and children, entreating, warning, encouraging, as the case demands.[48]

When the leader makes personal visits, the following benefits can be achieved:

- *The member feels valued as an individual,* not just part of a crowd.
- *Personal needs of members are identified and addressed,* fostering a sense of care and support.
- *Relationships with members deepen and strengthen,* enhancing trust and influence.
- *The bond between the member and the church is fortified,* creating a sense of belonging.
- *Faith is reinforced and doubts are clarified,* providing spiritual encouragement.
- *Important decisions are discussed and supported,* guiding members in their spiritual journey.

This approach not only nurtures individual growth but also strengthens the unity and spiritual health of the entire congregation.

---

[48]Ellen G. White, Evangelism (Doral, FL: APIA, 1994), 346. The quote is taken from an article in Signs of the Times, January 28, 1886.

3   Teach.

The The leader must teach the new disciple personally and, at times accompany them to gatherings where they can further learn. Additionally, the leader should create opportunities for hands-on learning experiences.

Scripture underscores the importance of the leader's teaching ability for effective leadership:

- "And a servant of the Lord must not quarrel but be gentle to all, able to teach, patient" (2 Timothy 2:24). Paul expects the Lord's servant to possess teaching skills.
- "A bishop then must be blameless, the husband of one wife, temperate sober-minded, of good behavior, hospitable, able to teach" (1 Timothy 3:2).
- "Holding fast the faithful word as he has been taught, that he may be able, by sound doctrine, both to exhort and convict those who contradict" (Titus 1:9).

4   Preach the Word.

The apostles and disciples received profound insights and powerful teachings from Christ, who shared the beliefs and principles of the kingdom of God, strengthening their faith and deepening their understanding of the kingdom. Similarly, through preaching, leaders should aim to transform members' worldviews, promoting growth in faith.

The apostle Paul expressed frustration over the Corinthian church members' lack of spiritual maturity despite being offered more substantial teachings. He remarked, "And I, brethren, could not speak to you as to spiritual people but as to carnal, as to babes in Christ. I fed you with milk and not with solid food; for until now you were not able to receive it, and even now you are still not able" (1 Corinthians 3:1-2).

Through profound, spiritually enriching preaching, the growth of disciples' faith and maturity is fostered. Many churches have disciples who remain spiritually immature because the topics of sermons do not promote their spiritual growth.

Model of a power ministry

What has been presented here as the leader's actions constitutes what we refer to as a *model of a power ministry*. This model emphasizes that effective leadership is not merely about managing tasks or fulfilling obligations. Instead, it centers on the transformative power of spiritual growth, deep personal connections, and a commitment to guiding members in their journey of discipleship.

In a power ministry, leaders are called not just to preach or teach but to actively demonstrate the power of the kingdom of God through prayer, personal example, visitation, mentoring, and fostering unity. It is a ministry that draws its strength from reliance on the Holy Spirit, aligning closely with the practices of the early church and the model Christ presented to His disciples.

This approach moves beyond traditional leadership methods, inviting leaders and congregations to participate in a ministry that truly impacts and transforms lives, building up the body of Christ in the spirit of service and devotion.

The exercise of this ministry empowers the leader to fulfill the mission of perfecting the saints for the work of ministry. This is God's plan.

It is necessary for the leader to understand both his mission and his commitment to God to put into practice the principles of a ministry of power. Through this, the edification of the body of Christ and the manifestation of the kingdom of God in His church can be achieved. Remember: God has chosen you to fulfill the critical mission of empowering each member as an instrument of the Holy Spirit in this time. It is the power of God conquering the darkness!

At the beginning of this chapter, we discussed the story of two congregations facing great challenges. What happened? Discipling and training new leaders not only multiplies the impact of our leadership but also develops new leaders to elevate congregations to a higher level of service to God. While I was there, I prayed for two things: "Lord, change the hearts of the leaders and members so they act differently, or bring in new leaders and members who will serve You according to Your heart." And God answered!

Assessment

To close this chapter, I present an evaluation of how this principle is applied in your ministry and congregation.

Evaluation of the Church and Leaders in the Implementation of the Discipleship Plan:

1.   Does the church have a plan to move members from believers to discipling leaders? Yes____ No____

2. Does the church assess each month the number of members involved in sharing the gospel or serving in various ministries? Yes____ No____

3. Are invitations made at each gathering to encourage all members to commit to growth as disciples? Yes____ No____

4. Are leaders engaging in prayer and fasting, visiting members monthly, teaching, and preaching the Word of God to help perfect believers? Yes____ No____

If you would like a recommended discipleship plan for your congregation, along with templates for evaluating the plan and additional materials, we invite you to join our training group of leaders committed to revival. You can register or complete the form with your information at the end of this book.

Now, the resurrection or revival of a church requires addressing an additional question: *How can we attract more people to our congregation?* The secret lies in the following pages. Once again, I offer my prayer to the Almighty, asking for His richest blessings upon you.

6

The leader's strategy: THE SECRET OF IMPACT

Can we truly be satisfied with what is happening? No, my heart tells me no. The Holy Spirit says no! Even though we act with a conviction to obey the Word of God, at times it feels almost like an illusion. That's why many, regardless of their position, would rather that things stay as they are. But do we genuinely believe what Scripture says? What commitment do we hold? Are we dedicated to position and status, or to the Word of God? These and other questions come to mind like waves crashing against my emotions, stirring and challenging me. Why? Because I must answer to God, because I must be true to my conscience, because how could I ever act against the best interests of the kingdom of God?

Therefore, in writing this book, I do so with a sincere desire to find others who will join in both prayer and action, so that the church may become what God desires it to be once again: light for the world! A people who illuminate the entire earth with the glory of God..

How did the church come to be what it is?

There Some, when analyzing this issue, recognize both the challenges that postmodern and secular society pose to Christianity and the fact that the regular activities of congregations often lack relevance for today's world. It is as if these congregations are too focused on speaking to themselves, resulting in a

119

disconnect from the outside world. This disconnect is evident in what we se< generations of young people leaving congregations or feeling no sense c identity with what the church offers.

Living in this bubble that separates us from the world and isolates us withi the "monastery" of our own concerns distances us from the personal interest of others, from the community, and from the surrounding world. Thi separation strips the church of its power and purpose. Beyond presenting th truth within its walls, the church must embody that truth, being light and salt i the world. Ellen White underscores that the mission of the church is to proclain the gospel to the world.[49] So how to do it if, in addition to losing the nex generation, we do not represent an answer for others?

There is no doubt that to address this dilemma, we must understand th environment in which we operate. Society today relativizes truth. This mean that not only does everyone hold their own version of truth based on persona experience, but the value of absolute truth has also lost significance Consequently, human rights, individualism, and freedom of choice dominat< our times.

If the church aspires to reclaim its role in your city or community, it mus remain faithful to God and His Word, committing to be the church God expects it to be once more. Luke described it this way:

- "Then the word of God spread, and the *number of the disciples multiplie< greatly* in Jerusalem, and a great many of the priests were obedient to the faith" (Acts 6:7, emphasis added).

---

[49]"The church is God's appointed agency for the salvation of men. It was organized for service, and its mission is *to carry the gospel to the world.* From the beginning it has been God's plan that through His church shall be reflected to the world His fulness and His sufficiency. The members of the church, those whom He has called out of darkness into His marvelous light, are to show forth His glory." White, The Acts of the Apostles, 9, emphasis added.

- "Then the churches throughout all Judea, Galilee, and Samaria had peace and were edified. And walking in the fear of the Lord and in the comfort of the Holy Spirit, *they were multiplied*" (Acts 9:31, emphasis added).

- "But the word of God *grew* and *multiplied*" (Acts 12:24, emphasis added).[50]

The challenge ahead may indeed demand great efforts, but it is precisely for this reason that you have arrived at this pivotal moment. Now is the time to make an impact in your community, to reach into secular societies, and to transcend cultural barriers.

Paul's example of bridging cultural gaps (1 Corinthians 9:20) and the Christians in Jerusalem who, forced from their comfort zones by persecution, spread the gospel to new places (Acts 8:4), stand as clear illustrations of the outward-reaching mission the church must embrace if it seeks to grow and multiply.

Christ has the secret!

In this sense, churches must grasp and apply Christ's greatest secret for reaching the multitudes and overcoming social, cultural, or ideological barriers. By adopting this principle in leadership, we can expand our ministry exponentially, elevating it to a new level.

Consider the impact of Christ's ministry. Crowds followed Him constantly! This response was undoubtedly due to the appeal of His message. Those who

---

[50]The impact of church growth is so notable that the citizens of Thessalonica affirm: "But when they did not find them, they dragged Jason and some brethren to the rulers of the city, crying out, "These who have turned the world upside down have come here too" (Acts 17:6).

heard Him testified that He spoke with authority. And they were correct—Christ's message was essential for reaching the multitudes.

Yet, Scripture and the Spirit of Prophecy reveal an even deeper secret to His success. Applying this secret will transform your church, enabling it to make the most profound impact it has ever experienced. Now is the congregation's opportunity to become truly relevant in the world.

Why did the crowds follow Christ? The Gospels address this question by describing the essence of His ministry. In the material below, we'll examine just one aspect of the three-part model that comprised the Lord's ministry. In the following verses, you'll observe two things: what Christ did and the specific focus of His work. I invite you to reflect deeply and pray over each of these passages as you read. Take your time.

Emphasis on healing of body and spirit

- And Jesus went about all Galilee, teaching in their synagogues, preaching the gospel of the kingdom, and *healing all kinds of sickness* and *all kinds of disease* among the people. Then His fame went throughout all Syria; and they brought to Him *all sick people* who were *afflicted with various diseases and torments*, and those who were *demon-possessed, epileptics, and paralytics*; and He *healed* them (Matthew 4:23-24, emphasis added).

- Then Jesus went about all the cities and villages, teaching in their synagogues, preaching the gospel of the kingdom, and *healing every sickness and every disease* among the people (Matthew 9:35, emphasis added).

- But when Jesus knew it, He withdrew from there. And great multitudes followed Him, and He *healed* them all (Matthew 12:15, emphasis added).

- However, the report went around concerning Him all the more; and great multitudes came together to hear, *and to be healed by Him of their infirmities* (Luke 5:15, emphasis added).

Emphasis on attention to people's needs

- For some thought, because Judas had the money box, that Jesus had said to him, "Buy those things we need for the feast," or that he should *give something to the poor* (John 13:29, emphasis added.)
- But when you give a feast, invite *the poor, the maimed, the lame, the blind*. And you will be blessed, because they cannot repay you; for you shall be repaid at the resurrection of the just (Luke 14:13-14, emphasis added).
- For I was hungry and *you gave Me food*; I was thirsty and *you gave Me drink*; I was a stranger and *you took Me* in; I *was* naked and *you clothed Me*; I was sick and *you visited Me*; I was in prison and *you came to Me* (Matthew 25:35-36, emphasis added).

Emphasis on restoring relationships and unity

- By this all will know that you are My disciples, *if you have love for one another* (John 13:35, emphasis added).
- They said to Him, "Why then did Moses command to give a certificate of divorce, and to put her away?" He said to them, "Moses, *because of the hardness of your hearts*, permitted you to divorce your wives, but *from the beginning it was not so*. And I say to you, whoever divorces his wife, except for sexual immorality, and marries another, commits adultery; and whoever marries her who is divorced commits adultery (Matthew 19:7-9, emphasis added).
- Jesus said to her, "Go, *call your husband*, and come here." (John 4:16, emphasis added).

- Therefore if you bring your gift to the altar, and there remember that your brother has something against you, leave your gift there before the altar, and go your way. First *be reconciled to your brother*, and then come and offer your gift (Matthew 5 :23-24, emphasis added).

- "You have heard that it was said to those of old, 'You shall not murder, and whoever murders will be in danger of the judgment.' But I say to you that whoever *is angry with his brother without a cause* shall be in danger of the judgment. And whoever *says to his brother, 'Raca!'* shall be in danger of the council. But whoever *says, 'You fool!'* shall be in danger of hell fire (Matthew 5:21-22).

- "You have heard that it was said, 'An eye for an eye and a tooth for a tooth.' But I tell *you not to resist an evil person.* But whoever slaps you on your right cheek, turn the other to him also. If anyone wants to sue you and take away your tunic, let him have your cloak also. And whoever compels you to go one mile, go with him two. Give to him who asks you, and from him who wants to borrow from you do not turn away (Matthew 5:38-42, emphasis added).

- You have heard that it was said, 'You shall love your neighbor and hate your enemy.']But I say to you, *love your enemies, bless those who curse you, do good to those who hate you, and pray for those who spitefully use you and persecute you,* that you may be sons of your Father in heaven; for He makes His sun rise on the evil and on the good, and sends rain on the just and on the unjust. *For if you love those who love you, what reward have you?* Do not even the tax collectors do the same? And if you greet your brethren only, what do you do more than others? Do not even the tax collectors do so? Therefore you shall be perfect, just as your Father in heaven is perfect (Matthew 5:43-48, emphasis added).

I confess that the message in these texts deeply impacts my heart, challenging both my thinking and my actions. It's impossible for me to envision the church without seeing myself within it. After all, as I am, so the congregation will be!

Understanding this truth in my own life reveals just how powerful Jesus' message truly was! In His sermons and personal interactions, He worked with remarkable dedication and wisdom to emphasize three key areas: health, family, and needs or finances.

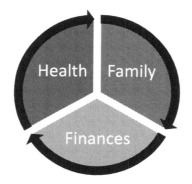

I can now understand the reason for the profound impact that Jesus and the early Christian church made in the first century. They had a powerful message and were a church that demonstrated the love of God. Could anything be more objective or striking than the description in the book of Acts? "There was therefore no one in need among them, because all those who owned land or houses sold them, brought the price of what was sold and laid it at the feet of the apostles. And it was distributed to each one as he had need" (Acts 4:34-35, emphasis added). People's needs were met.

The gospels clearly reveal how addressing needs amplified the impact of Christ's ministry.

Texts from the multitudes who followed Christ	
Matthew 4:25	"Great multitudes followed Him—from Galilee, and from Decapolis, Jerusalem, Judea, and beyond the Jordan."
Matthew 8:1	"When He had come down from the mountain, great multitudes followed Him."
Matthew 12:15	"But when Jesus knew it, He withdrew from there. And great multitudes followed Him, and He healed them all."
Mark 3:7	"But Jesus withdrew with His disciples to the sea. And a great multitude from Galilee followed Him, and from Judea."
Mark 5:24	"So Jesus went with him, and a great multitude followed Him and thronged Him."
Luke 6:17	"And He came down with them and stood on a level place with a crowd of His disciples and a great multitude of people from all Judea and Jerusalem, and from the seacoast of Tyre and Sidon, who came to hear Him and be healed of their diseases."
John 6:2	"Then a great multitude followed Him, because they saw His signs which He performed on those who were diseased."
Matthew 9:36	"But when He saw the multitudes, He was moved with compassion for them, because they were weary and scattered, like sheep having no shepherd."
Matthew 15:30	"Then great multitudes came to Him, having with them the lame, blind, mute, maimed, and many others; and they laid them down at Jesus' feet, and He healed them."
Luke 5:15	"However, the report went around concerning Him all the more; and great multitudes came together to hear, and to be healed by Him of their infirmities."
John 12:12-13	"The next day a great multitude that had come to the feast, when they heard that Jesus was coming to Jerusalem, took branches of palm trees and went out to meet Him, and cried out: 'Hosanna! 'Blessed is He who comes in the name of the Lord!' The King of Israel!'"

The expressions "many people," "great multitude," and "the multitudes" clearly illustrate that Jesus' ministry disrupted the neighborhood, town, region, country, and even countries that heard about Christ and His work. Understanding this, Ellen White emphasized that His method should be applied by congregations and followers of Jesus today, if we hope to see similarly successful results in our ministries. "Christ's method alone will give true success in reaching the people. The Saviour mingled with men as one who desired their good. He showed His sympathy for them, ministered to their needs, and won their confidence. Then He bade them, "Follow me."[51]

We must fully understand that Christ's method *focused* on meeting people's needs, not merely on sharing the message with them. He embodied the gospel, which is the challenge for today's church if it hopes to attract "many people," "multitudes," "great multitudes"—just as those who followed the Lord.

For anyone doubting that this applies to us, let me remind you of Christ's invitation to follow His example and believe in Him so that our ministry might mirror His victories. John recorded Jesus' promise: "Most assuredly, I say to you, he who believes in Me, *the works that I do he will do also; and greater works than these he will do, because I go to My Father.* And whatever you ask in My name, that I will do, that the Father may be glorified in the Son" (John 14:12,13, emphasis added).

So, what is the church to do?

Intentional Action Ministries

It is important to highlight that when we talk about ministry, it's not about a single activity but a continuous service of the church within a given period. Ministry is not an occasional program created to meet a requirement or quiet our conscience; that's not what God expects. Ministry is a set of intentional

---

[51]Ellen G. White, Maranatha: The Lord is Coming! (Doral, FL: APIA, 2008), 103.

actions carried out consistently—every week, biweekly, or at least monthly. It'
not about promoting ourselves or the church with a picture to show how goo
we are, but about glorifying God.

In this sense, ministry is:

1. Bringing the kingdom of God close to people who need t
    witness God's response to their need (Matthew 10:7).
2. A commitment to the person, not just to an event (Matthev
    25:35-36).
3. Transformational rather than transactional (Luke 10:9).
4. Done for Christ and for the love of Christ, not for ourselve
    (John 14:15).
5. Embodying Christ, becoming His hands and feet on this earth
    (John 14:12).
6. A lifestyle, something that is lived and demonstrated constantl
    (Matthew 5:14-16).

A comprehensive study of each of these points would require more time
and space than we have here. However, for establishing such a ministry
especially in regard to the first point, it will be crucial to consider at least fou
aspects for those facing this challenge. (See figure on the next page.)

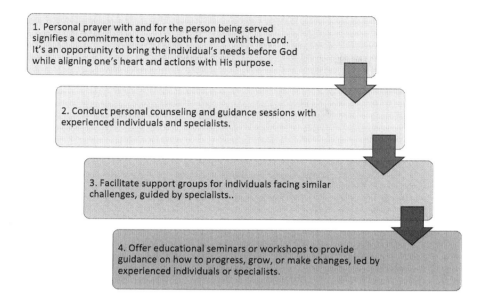

1. Personal prayer with and for the person being served signifies a commitment to work both for and with the Lord. It's an opportunity to bring the individual's needs before God while aligning one's heart and actions with His purpose.

2. Conduct personal counseling and guidance sessions with experienced individuals and specialists.

3. Facilitate support groups for individuals facing similar challenges, guided by specialists..

4. Offer educational seminars or workshops to provide guidance on how to progress, grow, or make changes, led by experienced individuals or specialists.

Finally, to achieve the objectives of these ministries within the local church, it is essential to unite the time and resources of all departments, following the example set by Jesus. We recommend that the church board establish a designated time each week for departmental operations and allocate at least 50% of resources toward the development of these ministries.

Ministry of health

For example, let's imagine we're in a small congregation with limited resources to establish a health ministry. Instead of waiting for more resources, start with something manageable. You could organize a simple Sunday morning or afternoon walk, open to both church members and the community. Just walk—yes, that's all to begin with!

Then, you can add some engaging elements: take participants' bloo
pressure at the start and end of the walk, have a short health talk, pray togethe
and invite everyone back for the next week.

Imagine after three months, participation has grown. You could then creat
posters to invite even more people for a larger walk event with prizes in ag
categories.

This walk could evolve further by incorporating health checks like glucos
monitoring, offering consultations, or concluding with a vegetarian meal. Yo
might even invite young people to join a church club or plan themed activitie
for families, like a special Christmas event, meals for mothers and fathers, o
other celebrations. Can you see the potential?

This health ministry could collaborate with other ministries—children
youth, men, women, family, or intercessory prayer—through shared or paralle
activities, coordinated under a unified vision.

For those who register as part of this transformation plan, we'll provide
additional ideas and guidance on implementing this and other initiatives
ensuring an impactful ministry growth journey.

Family ministry

A A group of departments can come together to support families in the
congregation by offering solutions one day a week, bridging the gap between
people's needs and the congregation's resources. Let's imagine this in a very
small congregation without any specialists. Starting simply, the couple with the
longest marriage could be assigned to coordinate this ministry. They might offer
support to men and women separately, create a plan for single-parent
households, or simply assist parents with guidance on raising their children.

Picture yourself walking on a Sunday morning with various people from
both the congregation and community, weaving through the neighborhood.
(Yes, this is the same activity from the health ministry that family ministry has

now joined.) As you walk together, you share conversations. Suddenly, someone opens up about wanting prayer for their child who is struggling at home. What an opportunity to invite them to the next family ministry gathering!

You might say, "Friend, how about joining us at our next meeting where we support families in prayer and share ways to navigate difficulties? I'd love for you to come along. If you're comfortable, you can even bring your daughter. We'll be there to support you both." Can you see it? We can position ourselves to meet people's real needs, right where they are!

Ministry of Finance

This This ministry is essential, focusing on two critical areas:

1. Meeting the needs of members and friends within small groups.
2. Teaching believers and community members to address their own needs by forming a covenant with God, wisely managing resources, and gaining the support and guidance to undertake projects that meet these needs.

To achieve these objectives, we recommend that fifty percent of the congregation's resources—after covering fixed expenses—be allocated to meeting members' and friends' needs through small groups. Remember, the other fifty percent is reserved for supporting all other ministries. (Refer to the figure below for a visual breakdown.)

131

Can Imagine the transformation in your congregation if the purpose of being the light of the world and the salt of the earth is truly lived out. You can probably see it vividly and feel a deep excitement, thinking about all that will unfold in your ministry and congregation. Remember Jesus' promise: "The works that I do, he will do also; and he will do even greater things, because I am going to the Father" (John 14:12). Do you believe it?

"Pastor, we're on several national news channels! The national newspaper and both regional and national radio stations are covering everything we're doing!" That leader was thrilled, his excitement palpable. He had never imagined his beloved church could have such a far-reaching impact in a country of 30 million people, but it was happening. In my heart, I thanked God for guiding us to invest a significant part of our resources in the implementation of the *Close to you* program.

The whole church united in action—helping families, children, and youth and delivering a message of hope. It was truly incredible! We had never experienced anything like it before. Christ's method is indeed the secret to success.

Assessment

To Here is an evaluation framework for applying Christ's method in your ministry and congregation. Use these questions to reflect on how effectively these principles are being implemented.

Evaluation of the Church and Leaders in Implementing the Christ-Method Plan

1.   Does your congregation have ministries or regular activities that align with Christ's method of service? Yes____ No____
2.   Is the health ministry active and happening each week in your congregation? Yes____ No____

3. Is the family ministry engaged in weekly activities, providing support and outreach to families within and beyond the congregation? Yes____ No____

4. Is the finance ministry operating weekly, offering guidance on resource management and wise stewardship? Yes____ No____

5. Is a record kept of those prayed for and cared for through the ministries, gathering members who serve, motivate, and support one another? Yes____ No____

6. Has the congregation's budget been adjusted to support the implementation of Christ's method in its ministries? Yes____ No____

In concluding this chapter, I encourage you to deeply reflect on these questions and the principles discussed. May they inspire you to lead a ministry that embodies biblical principles in a way that is impactful, relevant, and dedicated to the mission Christ entrusted to us. I continue to pray that you join in this mission with commitment and faith.

CONCLUSION

What have you learned? Is there something you need to do? What decisions and actions will you take moving forward? What God reveals to us is a great light, guiding our path with His pleasing and perfect will.

My prayer is that each solution to the challenges you and your congregation face has found an answer in these chapters, and that the journey you embark on from today will be the result of a transforming experience through the Holy Spirit, "by the renewing of your mind" (Romans 12:2).

We know that continuing the same approach will not yield different results. Now, we also know the five guiding principles that will lead us toward a renewed church, growing members, victories over challenges, the multiplication of committed disciples, and a community impact strategy like never before.

This journey begins in your spirit and moves through your heart. You have grasped the spiritual battle and the focus your leadership needs to complete the strategy. I am deeply grateful to God for the opportunity to write this, and for you to read it. The rest is in His hands, for we know that without His grace, we receive nothing. Amen. Let us have faith!

BEFORE YOU GO...

I would like to say thank you for buying this book, for reading it to the end. Now I would like to ask you a favor: Be part of the leadership development community by sending an email to:contacto@josneyrodriguez.com. We will be sending you information about upcoming materials and events.

Don't forget to leave your comment about the book:

Thanks again!

No more frustrated leaders and lifeless churches

ABOUT THE AUTHOR

Dr. Josney Rodríguez enjoys training leaders, pointing out on the horizon the dawn of new postmodern and biblical management and leadership. For more than 33 years he has dedicated himself to sharing seminars with leaders in more than 42 countries in America, and teaching academic instruction classes in master's and doctoral degrees. Furthermore, he accompanies and supports all those who are willing and committed in their professional, ecclesiastical and spiritual formation of their leadership and personal life, using all possible social means to achieve this important purpose as human beings and servants of God. We invite you to be part of those who believe in spiritual leadership without limits.

Web page:

Youtube:	**JosneyRodriguez**
Instagram:	**RodriguezJosney**
Twitter:	**JosneyRodriguez**
Facebook:	**JosneyDavidRodriguez**

EXHIBIT: Discipleship Plan

No more frustrated leaders and lifeless churches

FIRST YEAR

Stage	Level	Period	Theoretical knowledge in weekly church meetings	Practical objectives in weekly activities	Assessment	Discipleship in action in the small group
			Responsible: Elder, small group leader and department directors			
new believer	First level	Six months	•Seven fundamental beliefs of the church •Knowledge of spiritual disciplines •The testimony •Method of Christ •Christian relief work	• Developing a Small Group and Church Ministry • Witnessing using Christ's method	Monthly Church Board Evaluation Weekly evaluation in areas of discipleship growth, and monthly with your leader	Accompany a brother in witnessing and small group
	Second level	Six months	•Learn the prophecies of the book of Daniel •personal evangelism	• Give Bible studies • Share the message at home or small group	Monthly Church Board Evaluation Weekly personal evaluation in areas of discipleship growth, and monthly with your leader	Share the message through Bible Studies in missionary couples

Take this time to review this section and understand how it can apply to your congregation. The two great challenges of this first year are: First, that the new disciple be able to share the gospel with other people and become a fisher of men. Secondly, that he participate in a ministry of service to those in need. It is important that these two aspects are first also practiced in the family.

SECOND YEAR

Stage	Level	Period	Theoretical knowledge in weekly church meetings	Practical objectives in weekly activities	Assessment	Discipleship in Action in the Small Group
Responsible: Elder, small group leader and Department Directors						
young believer	Third level	Six months	• Class to learn from the book of Revelation • Public evangelism	• Participate in a campaign and give a message in the small group	Monthly Church Board Evaluation Weekly evaluation in areas of discipleship growth, and monthly with your leader	Preach sermons or actively participate in a campaign
	Room level	Six months	• Learn to answer questions • Learn Small Group Leadership	• Start a small group	Assessment Monthly Church Board Evaluation Weekly personal evaluation in areas of discipleship growth, and monthly with your leader	Be an associate leader of a new group

In this second year the double objective consists first of all: learning to preach; and secondly: knowing how to be a small group leader. Let's take time to evaluate our own spiritual growth and make the decision to commit to the growth of our actions in the Holy Spirit.

THIRD YEAR

Stage	Level	Period	Theoretical knowledge in weekly church meetings	Practical objectives in weekly activities	Assessment	Discipleship in action in the small group
Responsible: Elder, small group leader and Department Directors						
	Fifth Level	Six months	• Ecclesiastical training class • Training of ministry leaders	• Training in ministries	Monthly Church Board Evaluation Weekly evaluation in areas of discipleship growth, and monthly with your leader	Being a small group ministry leader
adult believer	Sixth level	Six months	• Review of everything learned • Give theoretical and practical discipleship classes • Make a personal growth plan for the coming years that includes growth in the 10 areas of spiritual growth	• Watch over the people under your responsibility, teaching and visiting them, developing a pastoral ministry	Monthly Church Board Evaluation Weekly personal evaluation in areas of discipleship growth, and monthly with your leader	Be a small group leader

No more frustrated leaders and lifeless churches

No more frustrated leaders and lifeless churches

No more frustrated leaders and lifeless churches

Made in the USA
Columbia, SC
16 November 2024

46130219R00083